Catholic for a Reason II

For behold, henceforth all generations will call me blessed; for he who is mighty has done great things for me, and holy is his name.

Luke 1:48-49

LEON J. SUPRENANT, JR.
EDITOR

Catholic for a Reason II

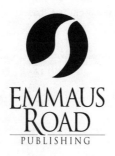

EMMAUS
ROAD
PUBLISHING

Nihil Obstat
Rev. James Dunfee
Censor Librorum

Imprimatur ✠
Most Rev. Gilbert I. Sheldon, D.D., D.Min.

© 2000 by Emmaus Road Publishing
All rights reserved.

Library of Congress (00-103064)
Published by
Emmaus Road Publishing
827 North Fourth Street
Steubenville, Ohio 43952
800-398-5470
www.emmausroad.org

Cover design by
Kinsey Advertising, Inc.
and Beth Hart

Published in the United States of America

ISBN 0-9663223-7-1

CONTENTS

Foreword

"Of Mary one can never speak enough." This saying was often quoted in the 1930s, 40s, and 50s in this country, a time when there was much Marian literature, both theological and devotional. The reason for making this point during these decades was not at all an *apologetic* one, as if one were answering those who might have been questioning the plethora of Marian literature, but rather to *encourage* many others to write about Our Lady and her role in our salvation.

In the 70s, 80s, and the early 90s, however, with a few exceptions, this phrase—"of Mary one can never speak enough"—tended to be quoted in an *apologetic* sense, the Marian author feeling the need to explain that we give our filial attention to Mary, of course, only insofar as she leads us to Christ, her Son.

Most of us have noticed that the past few years have brought a resurgence in Marian interest and devotion—hearkening back to the unquestioning love for Mary characteristic of the preconciliar years, but at the same time drawing upon the glorious teaching of Vatican II on Mary found in *Lumen Gentium*. For examples one need only look at the Marian Congresses being held around the country, the Rosary rallies, or the revitalized and newly active World Apostolate of Fatima. The list could go on and on.

This recent resurgence in Marian spirituality is cogently illustrated by the appearance of the book you have in your hands. For this outstanding treatise, we rejoice with a joy reflective of the Magnificat of Our Blessed Lady!

These few words of mine, then, serve as prologue to the wealth awaiting you in this book. I can think of no more fitting way to conclude these introductory comments than with some lines in praise of Mary found in *The Canterbury Tales*. These lines from the prologue to "The Prioress' Tale" ask Mary's blessing and enlightenment, in retrospect, for the authors whose treatises grace the following pages:

> O mother-maid! O maiden-mother free!
> O bush unburned, burning in Moses' sight,
> That down didst draw, with thine humility,
> The spirit of God within thee to alight,
> Out of whose virtue, when His will made bright
> Thine heart, the Father's wisdom came to birth—
> Now help my tale to honor thee on earth!
>
> Lady, thy goodness and thy shining glory,
> Thy virtue and thy great humility,
> No learned tongue can ever put in story,
> For sometimes, lady, ere we pray to thee,
> Thou hast foreseen, in thy benignity,
> And by thine intercession gett'st us light
> That to thy dear Son guides our feet aright.
>
> O blessed queen, so feeble is my wit
> To utter thy surpassing worthiness,
> I cannot well sustain the weight of it,
> But like a child twelve months of age or less,
> That scarce a word or two can well express,

So am I now; therefore I pray of you,
Guide well my song that I shall say of you.

Mary has heard our prayer; it is she who gives this book to you.

†James S. Sullivan
Bishop of Fargo

Abbreviations

THE OLD TESTAMENT

Gen.	Genesis
Ex.	Exodus
Lev.	Leviticus
Num.	Numbers
Deut.	Deuteronomy
Josh.	Joshua
Judg.	Judges
Ruth	Ruth
1 Sam.	1 Samuel
2 Sam.	2 Samuel
1 Kings	1 Kings
2 Kings	2 Kings
1 Chron.	1 Chronicles
2 Chron.	2 Chronicles
Ezra	Ezra
Neh.	Nehemiah
Tob.	Tobit
Jud.	Judith
Esther	Esther
Job	Job
Ps.	Psalms
Prov.	Proverbs
Eccles.	Ecclesiastes
Song	Song of Solomon
Wis.	Wisdom
Sir.	Sirach (Ecclesiasticus)
Is.	Isaiah
Jer.	Jeremiah
Lam.	Lamentations
Bar.	Baruch
Ezek.	Ezekiel
Dan.	Daniel
Hos.	Hosea

Joel	Joel
Amos	Amos
Obad.	Obadiah
Jon.	Jonah
Mic.	Micah
Nahum	Nahum
Hab.	Habakkuk
Zeph.	Zephaniah
Hag.	Haggai
Zech.	Zechariah
Mal.	Malachi
1 Mac.	1 Maccabees
2 Mac.	2 Maccabees

THE NEW TESTAMENT

Mt.	Matthew
Mk.	Mark
Lk.	Luke
Jn.	John
Acts	Acts of the Apostles
Rom.	Romans
1 Cor.	1 Corinthians
2 Cor.	2 Corinthians
Gal.	Galatians
Eph.	Ephesians
Phil.	Philippians
Col.	Colossians
1 Thess.	1 Thessalonians
2 Thess.	2 Thessalonians
1 Tim.	1 Timothy
2 Tim.	2 Timothy
Tit.	Titus
Philem.	Philemon
Heb.	Hebrews
Jas.	James

1 Pet.	1 Peter
2 Pet.	2 Peter
1 Jn.	1 John
2 Jn.	2 John
3 Jn.	3 John
Jude	Jude
Rev.	Revelation (Apocalypse)

DOCUMENTS OF VATICAN II

SC   Constitution on the Sacred Liturgy
(*Sacrosanctum Concilium*), December 4, 1963

IM   Decree on the Means of Social Communication
(*Inter Mirifica*), December 4, 1963

LG   Dogmatic Constitution on the Church
(*Lumen Gentium*), November 21, 1964

OE   Decree on the Catholic Eastern Churches
(*Orientalium Ecclesiarum*), November 21, 1964

UR   Decree on Ecumenism
(*Unitatis Redintegratio*), November 21, 1964

CD   Decree on the Pastoral Office of Bishops in the Church
(*Christus Dominus*), October 28, 1965

PC   Decree on the Up-to-Date Renewal of Religious Life
(*Perfectae Caritatis*), October 28, 1965

OT   Decree on the Training of Priests
(*Optatam Totius*), October 28, 1965

GE   Declaration on Christian Education
(*Gravissimum Educationis*), October 28, 1965

NA   Declaration on the Relation of the Church to Non-
Christian Religions (*Nostra Aetate*), October 28, 1965

DV   Dogmatic Constitution on Divine Revelation
(*Dei Verbum*), November 18, 1965

AA   Decree on the Apostolate of Lay People
(*Apostolicam Actuositatem*), November 18, 1965

DH   Declaration on Religious Liberty
(*Dignitatis Humanae*), December 7, 1965

AG   Decree on the Church's Missionary Activity
       (*Ad Gentes Divinitus*), December 7, 1965
PO   Decree on the Ministry and Life of Priests
       (*Presbyterorum Ordinis*), December 7, 1965
GS   Pastoral Constitution on the Church in the Modern
       World (*Gaudium et Spes*), December 7, 1965

CATECHISM OF THE CATHOLIC CHURCH

Throughout the text, the *Catechism of the Catholic Church* (United States Catholic Conference–Libreria Editrice Vaticana, 1994, as revised in the 1997 Latin typical edition) will be cited simply as "Catechism."

CHAPTER I

She Gave the Word Flesh

SCOTT HAHN

D ivine providence often furnishes Catholic converts with ironic stories about the twists and turns on their journeys home to the Catholic Church. In my case, as a former Protestant minister with deep anti-Catholic convictions, it was my Saul-like crusade against Mary that was wondrously transformed by God's grace into a deep filial love for the Mother of God. As they say, the bigger they come, the harder they fall—in love.

"Over My Dead Calvinist Body!"

For many years, I considered Marian doctrine and devotion to be symptomatic of a mortal infection within Catholics; indeed, it represented what was most wrong with Catholicism. Paradoxically, my former anti-Marian views have resulted in an appreciation for the common objections frequently raised against the Church's teachings about Mary.

When I was an Evangelical, the one overarching reason why I opposed Catholic teaching about Mary was that I believed that it undermined the perfect work of Christ and robbed Him of His glory. Today, the one overarching reason why I embrace the Church's teaching is that I now see Mary as the perfect work of Christ and the greatest revelation of His glory. She no more steals the Son's glory than the moon steals the sun's.

In view of the potholes and detours I have encountered along the road to Rome, perhaps it would be useful to clarify how this Evangelical came to accept the Church's teachings.

Drawing a Bead

I recall the days when I was still in a sort of spiritual "no man's land" between my Evangelical past and my eventual home with Rome. I could no longer honestly preach as a Protestant minister, but I still had lingering doubts about Catholic doctrine. One by one, however, my doubts fell away as I studied Catholic theology and tradition until, finally, only the Marian doctrines remained.

These were substantial obstacles for me. Cradle Catholics often have no idea of the repugnance "Bible Christians" feel for Marian doctrines and devotions. It was then that someone mailed me a plastic rosary. As I opened the package, I felt I was facing the toughest obstacle of all. Yet, by that time, so many doctrines of the Catholic Church had proven to be biblically sound that I decided to step out in faith on this one. I began, hesitatingly, to pray my first Rosary, offering it for a specific intention, a situation that seemed hopeless by human standards.

Wonder of wonders, my prayers were answered. That seemingly impossible situation was completely reversed. This was success far beyond my expectations. I was astonished.

Still, a greater miracle was under way, one that was revealed to me by a conversation with an old friend from college. He knew me when I was most ardently anti-Catholic, and he had been watching my Romeward journey with increasing alarm. One day he called and cut right to the point: "So, Scott, are you worshipping Mary yet?"

"C'mon, Chris. You know that Catholics don't worship Mary. They simply venerate her."

"Really, Scott, what's the difference? There's no biblical basis either way."

I began fingering my rosary beads, and I was emboldened. I proceeded on biblical principles. First, I reminded Chris that, as a man, Christ fulfilled God's law perfectly, including the commandment to honor one's father and mother. The Hebrew word for honor, *kabbed*, literally means "to glorify." So Christ didn't just honor His Heavenly Father. He also perfectly honored His earthly mother, Mary, by bestowing His own divine glory upon her.

Our veneration of Mary, then, is an essential part of our imitation of Christ. We follow Him not just by honoring our own mothers, but also by honoring whomever He honors—and with the same honor that He bestows.

Here was the greater miracle I gained through the Rosary. From that moment, I sensed how praying the beads deepened my own theological penetration of Scripture. Mary was no longer an obstacle to faith; she was opening its mysteries to me.

The Gospel of Jesus Embodied in Mary

Jesus announced the Gospel, and then proceeded to fulfill it. But the Gospel did not change the Second Person of the Trinity. The eternal Son did not gain a single drop of glory for Himself—after living, dying, and rising as man—that He lacked beforehand. God did not create and redeem the world in order to *get* more glory, but rather to *give* it. There is no tug-of-war between the Creator and His creatures. The Father made and redeemed us through the Son and the Spirit, but They did it for us—starting with Mary, in whom it was accomplished not only first, but best.

Do we detract from Christ's finished work by affirming its perfect realization in Mary? On the contrary, we celebrate His work precisely by focusing our attention on the human person who manifests it most perfectly.

Mary is not God, but she is the Mother of God. She is only a creature, but she is God's greatest creation. Just as artists long to paint one masterpiece among their many works, so Jesus made His mother to be His greatest masterpiece. To continue the metaphor: No artist is offended when we praise his greatest work. In fact, he might be offended if we don't. To affirm the truth about Mary does not detract from Jesus, although *not* to affirm it could.

Mary is directly related to God by a natural bond of covenant kinship, as the Mother of Jesus, to whom she gave her own flesh and blood. This bond is what enables us to share the New Covenant grace of Christ by adoption. Furthermore, Jesus is legally bound by His Father's law ("Honor your father and mother") to share His honor with Mary, as her Son. Indeed, He fulfilled this law more perfectly than any son has ever done, by bestowing the gift of His divine glory upon her. And we are simply called to imitate Him.

We Are Family

Pope John Paul II has stated: "God in His deepest mystery is not a solitude, but a family, since He has in Himself fatherhood, sonship, and the essence of the family, which is love."[1] The work of salvation is the work of all three Persons of the Holy Trinity. Our redemption thus assumes Trinitarian and family proportions.

The First Person of the Trinity is now Our Father (cf. Jn. 20:17) because of the saving work of the Son, who is the "the first-born among many brethren" (Rom. 8:29), and so the Holy Spirit is "the spirit of sonship," who causes us to cry "Abba! Father!" (Rom. 8:15). This is what is so distinctive about the Christian religion: It is the Gospel of God's sharing His family life and love with mankind.

The story of our redemption, then, unfolds precisely as a family history, with a Father, an older Brother, and many siblings, united in a bond of love. Only one more person remains to make

---

[1] *Puebla: A Pilgrimage of Faith* (Boston: Daughters of St. Paul, 1979), 86.

the correspondence perfect: a mother. No family is complete without a loving mother, and every motherless family feels this absence as an aching need. Our need for a mother is implicit even in the word Saint Paul uses to describe our relationship with one another. We are "brethren"—in Greek, *adelphoi*, meaning "from the womb." As brothers in Jesus Christ, we share a common mother, and she is His own mother.

Thus the correspondence is complete. God's family is perfect, lacking nothing. In His tender mercy, God gave us a mother. And it all began with the gift of Mary as mother: She obeyed the Father by bearing His Son in the power of the Holy Spirit—for us.

Christmas' Eve

Mary's role is not merely incidental to Jesus' life. We find it foreshadowed in the first pages of the Old Testament, in the life of Eve, the mother of all the living. We find it, too, in the last pages of the New Testament, in the Book of Revelation, where Mary is depicted symbolically as the Ark of the New Covenant, the vessel chosen to bear the baby who was our Redeemer (Rev. 11:19 *et seq.*). By her "yes" to God, Mary cooperated in the redemption of Eve's children, through the reversal of Eve's sin.

With stunning clarity, Saint Irenaeus, in the second century, described Mary's role in God's overarching plan:

> By disobeying, [Eve] became the cause of death for herself and for the whole human race. In the same way, Mary, though she also had a husband, was still a virgin, and by obeying, she became the cause of salvation for herself and for the whole human race. . . . The knot of Eve's disobedience was untied by Mary's obedience. What Eve bound through her unbelief, Mary loosed by her faith.[2]

[2] Saint Irenaeus of Lyons, *Adversus Haereses* (*Against Heresies*), 3, 22, as quoted in Luigi Gambero, S.M., *Mary and the Fathers of the Church* (San Francisco: Ignatius Press, 1999), 54. See also Catechism, no. 494.

A Mother's Work Is Never Done

The history of redemption is a story that involves human participation. The Apostle Paul spoke of this mystery when he stated, "We are God's co-workers" (1 Cor. 3:9, New American Bible). How is this? Can't God get the job done Himself? Of course He can. But since He is a Father, His job is to raise up mature sons and daughters by making us co-workers. And His work is our redemption, which He shared in an unparalleled way with Mary—to whom God entrusted such tasks as feeding His Son with her own milk, singing Him to sleep, and accompanying Him all the way to the Cross where she gave her sorrowful yes to His self-offering. In short, the Father willed that His Son's entire existence as a man would hinge, so to speak, upon the ongoing *fiat* of Mary. Can there be a more intimate "co-worker"?

Being a disciple, a co-worker with Jesus, takes effort. At times, it takes suffering. One passage that seemed to have escaped my attention as a Protestant was Saint Paul's rather curious line, "I rejoice in my sufferings for your sake, and in my flesh I complete what is lacking in Christ's afflictions for the sake of his body, that is, the church" (Col. 1:24). Cradle Catholics may remember with some fondness being told (in the event of an unsuccessful team tryout, a skinned knee, or a broken heart) to "offer it up." This simple phrase holds the key that unlocks the mystery of our co-redemption. By consciously uniting our sufferings to Our Lord's redemptive sufferings, we become co-workers. By uniting her heart to His, especially at Calvary, the Blessed Mother became the co-worker *par excellence*.

This understanding was summarized at Vatican II (1962-65):

> This motherhood of Mary in the order of grace continues uninterruptedly from the consent which she loyally gave at the Annunciation and which she sustained without wavering beneath the cross, until the eternal fulfillment of all the elect (LG 62; cf. Catechism, no. 969).

However, Mary's divine maternity did not end with her Son's Resurrection and Ascension, nor even after her Assumption, as *Lumen Gentium* continues:

> Taken up to heaven she did not lay aside this saving office but by her manifold intercession continues to bring us the gifts of eternal salvation. . . . Therefore the Blessed Virgin is invoked in the Church under the titles of Advocate, Helper, Benefactress, and Mediatrix (*ibid.*).

It is significant that Vatican II and the Catechism describe Mary's divine motherhood as a "saving office," which provides the basis for her rather remarkable titles. But what is meant by the phrase "saving office"?

Mother in the Middle

A well-trained theologian, Pope John Paul II has introduced the compact phrase "maternal mediation" into the Church's theological vocabulary. And it seems to capture the very heart of Marian doctrine and devotion.

As an Evangelical, I used to rush to the one verse that seemed to snuff out this seemingly heretical spark: Saint Paul's categorical assertion that Christ is the only "mediator between God and men" (1 Tim. 2:5). How dare we refer to Mary's maternal mediation!

First, the Greek word used here for "one" is *eis*, which means "first" or "primary," not *monos*, which means "only" or "sole." Just as there is one mediator, there is also one divine sonship, which we all share—by way of participation—with Christ (*filii in Filio*, sons in the Son). Christ's mediation does not exclude Mary's, but rather establishes it, by way of her participation.

Furthermore, the Epistle to the Hebrews explains Christ's high priesthood in terms of His being the first-born Son of God (Heb. 1:5–2:17), which serves as the basis for our divine sonship (Heb. 2:10-17), as well as our priestly sanctity and service (cf. Heb. 13:10-16; 1 Pet. 2:5). Once again, there is no tug-of-war between Christ's one priesthood and our participation in it.

As first-born Son in God's family, Jesus mediates as the High Priest between the Father and His children, whereas Mary mediates as Queen Mother (cf. 1 Kings 2:19; Rev. 12:1-17). This is what her maternal mediation is all about. For the Father, Mary mothers the Son. For us sinners, she mothers our Savior. And for her Son, she mothers His siblings. When it comes to Mary's role in God's saving plan, "mother" is not only a noun, but a verb, and hence an office.

As the Mother of God and His children, Mary shows us how to glorify the Father, not by groveling, but by receiving the gift of His Son in the fullness of the Spirit. That is how God's sovereign grace enables us to share in His glory, and so become "partakers of the divine nature" (2 Pet. 1:4). So if you want to judge how well a person grasps the Gospel in its essence, find out how much they make of having God as their Father—and Mary as their mother.

Christ Won Her Winning Ways

The theological concept of *merit* is frequently misunderstood by Catholics and Protestants alike. If merit is understood as a purely economic term, it's untrue and offensive; but if it is understood in a familial sense, it is as natural as an inheritance, or an allowance. In other words, as children in God's family, we merit as a child earns dessert—by eating everything on his plate. What father begrudges his kids the gifts he gives them, or resents those whom he rewards? As Saint Augustine wrote: "[I]n crowning their merits you are crowning your own gifts" (as quoted in Catechism, no. 2006).

According to the Catechism, "God's fatherly action" enables us to merit:

> Filial adoption, in making us partakers by grace in the divine nature, can bestow *true merit* on us as a result of God's gratuitous justice. This is our right by grace, the full right of love, making us "co-heirs" with Christ (Catechism, no. 2009, original emphasis).

Christ has merited our capacity to merit—which He confers on us with the grace of His divine sonship and the life of His Spirit. Indeed, Jesus did not merit a single thing for Himself, since there was nothing He needed. Thus, He only merits according to our need.

Where does God the Father show the world just how much His Son really merited? In each one of us, to be sure, but most of all in Mary. Unlike the rest of us—in whom there is often a yawning gap between what we want and what God wants—with Mary there is no gap. By the gift of an unsurpassed grace, Mary attained the goal of the covenant: a perfect interpersonal union of divine and human wills. With Mary, the ideal and real are one and the same.

Bad for Ecumenism?

As I said at the beginning of this chapter, for "Bible Christians," Marian doctrines are perhaps the most frightening aspect of Catholicism. Some Catholics recognize this and respond by downplaying all things Marian—at least when they're dealing with Protestants—for fear that they'll offend or scare away a friend who's drawing near. Yet, as we have seen, the Marian doctrines are not something incidental to our faith; they touch upon the central truths. They affect our relationship with God, with the Church, and with one another. Moreover, two of these Marian teachings have, in recent times, been solemnly defined as dogmas: the Immaculate Conception (1854) and the Assumption (1950). By these extraordinary actions, the Church seems to be saying, quite clearly, that today is no time to hide our mother away.

Throughout the history of the Church, the definition of dogmas has stimulated the apostolic and theological energies of some of the best minds, especially when a definition becomes the subject of controversy. More recently, many Protestants—including the late Max Thurian of the ecumenical community in Taizé, France—objected strenuously after hearing rumors that Pope Pius XII was about to define the dogma of Mary's bodily

Assumption into heaven at the end of her earthly life. After all, where does the Assumption appear in the Bible? Yet Pope Pius XII would indeed define the dogma, and Max Thurian would himself, eventually, enter the Catholic Church, be ordained a priest, and pass from this life on August 15, 1996, the Solemnity of the Assumption.

Authentic ecumenical progress is not simply the result of our own human energies. Nor is it advanced by compromise on either side. Pope John Paul II wrote:

> Here it is not a question of altering the deposit of faith, changing the meaning of dogmas, eliminating essential words from them, accommodating truth to the preferences of a particular age. . . . The unity willed by God can be attained only by the adherence of all to the content of revealed faith in its entirety.[3]

Ecumenical unity thus requires a special grace and the work of God, who acts for the sake of His family. Accordingly, we should not expect Him to work *apart from* but *through* the mother He gave us to serve as the symbol and source of family unity.

It may be significant, in this connection, that experts often trace the rise of Catholic ecumenism back to the early 1950s. This immediately followed the definition of the Assumption and the celebration of a Marian Year in 1954 as the centenary of the definition of the Immaculate Conception. If there ever was a time when Catholic ecumenism could have been expected to go into a deep-freeze, it would have been that decade. But instead of a chill, Catholics and Protestants experienced the start of a great thaw.

As we begin the third millennium, I believe that God wants to use Mary to bring a deep grace of conversion to all Christendom, not only Protestant and Orthodox, but Catholic as well. This fits with the Holy Father's call for authentic ecumenism to be based

---

[3] Encyclical Letter On Commitment to Ecumenism *Ut Unum Sint* (1995), no. 18.

on a "dialogue of conversion."[4] Such conversion might seem improbable by human standards, but it's one that I know can take place, because I have known it myself as a singular grace from God, mediated by His mother.

We can begin this dialogue now, if only we speak with the courage of our convictions. As we celebrate the jubilee of Christ's birth from Mary, how fitting that we turn to her, who gave the Word flesh.

Scott Hahn received his doctorate in theology from Marquette University in Milwaukee, Wisconsin, and is a professor of theology at Franciscan University of Steubenville. He is an internationally known Catholic lecturer and apologist. In addition to the Catholic for a Reason *series, his books include* The Lamb's Supper: The Mass as Heaven on Earth *(Doubleday),* A Father Who Keeps His Promises: God's Covenant Love in Scripture *(Servant Books) and* Rome Sweet Home *(Ignatius Press), which he coauthored with his wife Kimberly.*

---

[4] *Ibid.*, no. 82.

CHAPTER II

Mary, Mary
Quite Contrary

CURTIS MARTIN

I still remember the night I left the Catholic Church. I was sitting in a room with some Christian friends of mine having an enjoyable discussion, and I remembered a joke that I thought I would share with them: One day Our Lord was confronted by the Pharisees with a woman who had been caught in adultery. They tested Jesus, saying, "Teacher, what should we do with her? The law of Moses says that she should be stoned. What do you say?" Jesus looked at the crowd and then looked mercifully at the woman. He turned back to the crowd and said, "Let the one among you who has no sin cast the first stone." As He turned back to the woman, a rock flew over His shoulder and hit the woman. Startled, Our Lord turned around and with a sense of surprise said, "Mother!"

I had told the joke before, and it had always gotten laughs, but this night was different. After a long and uncomfortable silence, one by one, my friends began to question why I believed what I believe. "Curtis, where in the Bible does it say that Mary has no sin?" I wasn't well trained in Scripture and couldn't remember exact passages. I responded, "Gee, I don't know. Do

you know where it is?" One after the other, my friends assured
me that nowhere does the Bible say that Mary is without sin. In
fact, they said, the Scriptures were clear that "all have sinned
and fall short of the glory of God" (Rom. 3:23) and "[n]one is
righteous, no, not one" (Rom. 3:10).

They began to shower me with a series of questions and
challenges about Mary: "Where in the Bible does it say she was
assumed into heaven? Don't you know that the Scriptures clearly
teach that there is only one mediator? Why do Catholics say that
Mary can hear our prayers? Catholics teach that Mary remained a
virgin and yet the Bible is clear that Jesus had brothers. Catholics
pray the Rosary and repeat the Hail Mary over and over again, and
yet Our Lord Himself condemned vain repetition in prayer. . . ."

My head was spinning. I didn't know how to respond. I felt
betrayed. In front of me were seven or eight of the most faithful,
consistent, Christian young adults I had ever met. All of them
flatly rejected the Catholic teachings on Mary. The evidence
seemed overwhelming. The Christians I knew who were prayerful,
who knew the Scriptures, who were committed to living lives of
integrity were all non-Catholic Christians, while my Catholic
friends with whom I had grown up all seemed to be struggling.
Most of them had stopped going to Mass. Few of them seemed
to believe what the Church taught, and I didn't know any who
could convincingly explain these teachings.

I began to think that Catholicism was an obstacle to coming
to know Christ. It wasn't that I had a problem with Mary. She
was the mother of Jesus and seemed to be a good Christian. I
had a problem with the Church's teachings about Mary. As I
began to have discussions with my Catholic friends, I started to
see that many of them also had difficulties with the Church's
teachings on Mary. I even developed a list of objections to many
of the Catholic Church's teachings, and particularly those concerning Mary—her role in salvation history and in the life of the
individual Christian.

As Catholics, we are sometimes overwhelmed by questions
about our faith. We need to take these questions seriously and

when we do, we will come to appreciate the truth, power, and beauty of the Catholic faith. As we look at some of the objections people have concerning the Church's teaching about Mary, we will see how a change of perspective based upon a faithful reading of Scripture can help us see that everything the Catholic Church teaches about Mary is true. But, before we look at the answers, let's take a look at some of the questions.

One Mediator?

Under the inspiration of the Holy Spirit, Saint Paul writes, "For there is one God, and there is one mediator between God and men, the man Christ Jesus" (1 Tim. 2:5). The Scriptures are so clear that there is one mediator. Why are Catholics so quick to add Mary and all of the saints as mediators? After my friends challenged me, I began to think that if Catholics would just read the Scriptures they would see that so much of what they believe openly contradicts the Word of God. I began to think that Catholic teaching was a perfect example of a sin that Saint Paul condemned:

> So they are without excuse; for although they knew God they did not honor him as God or give thanks to him, but they became futile in their thinking and their senseless minds were darkened. Claiming to be wise, they became fools, and exchanged the glory of the immortal God for images resembling mortal man (Rom. 1:20-23).

Upstaging God?

Christians have been called to give glory and praise to God. We are called to love the Lord Our God with all our heart, mind, soul, and strength. Yet it appeared to me that Catholics were a house divided as they spent their energies praising and honoring Mary and other saints. Catholics seemed to blur the teaching of Scripture that draws such a clear distinction between God and man. Marian devotions seemed to fall right into the idolatry which humanity is so prone to accept.

For example, when Saint Peter entered the house of Cornelius, Cornelius fell on his feet and worshipped him. But Peter said, "Stand up; I too am a man" (Acts 10:26). Even the Apostle John seems to be prone to this same error when in the Book of Revelation he meets an angel. John says,

> I fell down at his feet to worship him, but he said to me, "You must not do that! I am a fellow servant with you and your brethren who hold the testimony of Jesus. Worship God" (Rev. 19:10).

I felt sure that if Mary could, she would tell Catholics the same thing: "Do not worship me—worship God." Catholic teaching seemed to contradict the spirit and the letter of Scripture. In a very real sense, I began to feel sorry for Mary. Scripture presents her as a humble handmaid of the Lord. I imagined that she was in anguish thinking of the poor, misguided Catholics who were directing their praise and worship to her rather than the God whom she had served so faithfully.

Mary the Virgin?

As a young Catholic, I had always been taught that Mary was ever-virgin, and that Jesus was her only Son. But as I began to read Scripture, I thought that this was another Catholic teaching that was apparently contradicted by what the Bible taught. "Is not this the carpenter's son? Is not his mother called Mary? And are not his brethren James and Joseph and Simon and Judas?" (Mt. 13:55). The Gospels don't hide Jesus' family. They even go so far as to name His brothers![1]

Saint Matthew does teach that Saint Joseph "knew her not until she had borne a son" (Mt. 1:25). Certainly Christians

---

[1] A more thorough reading would also show that at least two of these four "brothers" have a different mother (cf. Mt. 27:56; Catechism, no. 500). It is actually our impoverished understanding of family that leads to our misreading of Scripture on this point. See chapter seven for more extensive treatment of Mary's Perpetual Virginity.

recognize the miraculous birth foretold at the Annunciation (Lk. 1:26-38) and thus acknowledge that Mary was the virgin mother of Jesus. But Scripture clearly teaches that Mary was a virgin *until* the birth of Christ (cf. Mt. 1:25). Why would Catholics be so foolish as to ignore Scripture and state that she remained a virgin afterwards? Similarly, Luke's Gospel mentions that Jesus is a first-born (Lk. 2:7). It seemed as if Catholics ignored the clear scriptural evidence in order to develop a mis-placed devotion to Mary.

Vain Repetition?

As if the excessive attention paid to the Mother of Christ were not enough, it appeared to me that Catholics moved beyond this in their devotional life. The classic example was the Rosary. Our Lord Himself teaches us how to pray in the Sermon on the Mount. He says that "in praying do not heap up empty phrases as the Gentiles do; for they think that they will be heard for their many words" (Mt. 6:7).

While I admittedly didn't know much about the Rosary, I remembered seeing people sitting in church with beads in their hands muttering over and over again "Hail Mary. . ." dozens and dozens of times. This seemed to be a classic example of the repetition that Our Lord so clearly condemned. I wanted to encourage my Catholic friends that they could speak openly and directly with Christ. Repeating this same prayer over and over again to Mary wouldn't get their prayers answered. Rather, I thought they needed to reject this unbiblical practice and go straight to the source: Jesus Christ, God Almighty.

Graven Images?

On top of all the other excesses in Marian devotion, Catholic churches and even Catholic homes were filled with statues of Mary. I could imagine that a Catholic would be unaware of some biblical teachings, because as a cradle Catholic I too was unfamiliar with so much of Scripture. But the rejection of graven images is not taken from some obscure biblical passage; it's right there in the Ten Commandments! Moses teaches:

> You shall have no other gods before me. You shall not make for yourself a graven image, or any likeness of anything that is in heaven above, or that is in the earth beneath, or that is in the water under the earth; you shall not bow down to them or serve them; for I the LORD your God am a jealous God (Ex. 20:3-5).

How far had Catholicism fallen? In my mind, the arguments became more and more clear all the time. I began to think that the reason I had not known Jesus more intimately as a young Catholic was because Catholicism had led me astray. The Bible itself warns the Church about what will happen if we shift attention away from Christ:

> I have this against you, that you have abandoned the love that you had at first. Remember then from what you have fallen, repent and do the works you did at first. If not, I will come to you and remove your lampstand from its place, unless you repent (Rev. 2:4-5).

I now thought that I had found the fatal flaw: The Catholic Church had slipped into error and lost Jesus, her first love.

Conceived Without Sin?

Another classic example of the confusion concerning Mary seemed to be the dogmatic teaching of the Catholic Church that she was conceived without sin. I think more Catholics would struggle with this teaching, but they mistakenly think that the Immaculate Conception refers to the beginning of the life of Jesus within the womb of Mary. The teaching actually affirms that Mary, from the first moment of *her* conception, in the womb of her mother Saint Ann, was free from original sin and all of its effects.

Catholics maintain that Mary was sinless even though Scripture teaches that "all have sinned and fall short of the glory of God" (Rom. 3:23). In this teaching more than anywhere else, it seemed to me that the Catholic Church was obviously trying to make Mary out to be a goddess—not a sinner like us in need of salvation, but someone free from sin, like God. It seemed that from the Catholic perspective, Jesus wasn't Mary's savior, but her partner. But Christ alone is the Savior of the whole world; "there is salvation in no one else" (Acts 4:12).

As I asked these questions, I didn't think I had anything against Mary. My love for Christ found me not fighting against Mary, but fighting for Christ against the Church's teachings about Mary. I wanted to respect, honor, and praise Jesus' unique role in salvation. How could I do that and be Catholic? As all of these issues swirled around in my mind, I found myself bewildered. How could I as a Christian love my Catholic family and friends? Obviously, I thought, I had to free them from this stockpile of error and confusion that seemed to keep them from a pure and simple relationship with Christ. Or did I?

On the Contrary

These questions and others like them deserve serious consideration. They are good questions and, if the Catholic Church can't provide a response, then her opponents are right: We should forsake the Catholic Church and follow Jesus. As Catholics, we need to take these questions seriously because there are sincere people both within and outside the Church who are kept from the fullness of the truth of Christ because they have not heard the Catholic response. These are good questions, and the Church has great answers!

You may be wondering why a Catholic would be willing to raise these questions.

The difference between a zealous anti-Catholic and a faithful Catholic is often not as great as it may seem. In his early days, Saint Paul was a zealous persecutor of the Church. In all sincerity, he viewed Christianity as an enemy of true religion, and so he eagerly sought to destroy the Church. Saint Paul's arguments were based on truth, but he was missing one fundamental truth: that Jesus Christ is God and the fulfillment of the Old Covenant.

When Jesus informed Saint Paul about that single, fundamental truth, Saint Paul experienced a radical conversion and became a great defender of Christianity and the Apostle to the Gentiles. He became part of the very foundation of the Church of Jesus Christ (cf. Eph. 2:20).

In the same way, those who, in all sincerity, find themselves rejecting the Church's teachings about the Blessed Virgin Mary are often only one step away from the fullness of the faith. Like Saint Paul, they think that they are sincerely fulfilling the will of God. As Catholics, it is our role to explain to them the salvation of Christ so that they might understand that the teachings about Mary do not take away from the glory of God, but manifest it. Just as she gave flesh to God the Son, she also gives flesh to His Gospel throughout the centuries.

Christ in Us

Our Evangelical friends rightly bring up the fact that "there is one mediator between God and men, the man Christ Jesus" (1 Tim. 2:5), but they fail to understand the power, depth, and nature of that mediation. Mary and the saints intercede for us not as other mediators separate and distinct from Christ, but as an extension of Christ's mediation. It was Jesus Himself who said, "Abide in me, and I in you. As the branch cannot bear fruit by itself, unless it abides in the vine, neither can you, unless you abide in me" (Jn. 15:4).

Jesus saves us by incorporating us into Himself, like a branch is united to a vine, so that there is no clear distinction as to where the vine ends and the branch begins. The branch only has life if it is united to the vine. This fundamental understanding changes everything. It takes the objections of our Evangelical brothers and sisters and the misunderstandings of our Catholic brothers and sisters and turns it completely around. Our Father is not in competition with us, as though He is honored only if we are not. God's victory is to share His goodness with us—He accomplishes His will when His love is manifested in our hearts. Our Father chooses to share His glory with His saints (cf. Rom. 8:29-30).

Through faith and Baptism, the Christian is intimately united with Christ. In fact, he or she begins to live *in* Christ. God's life and love within the heart and soul of the believer allows each of us to participate in His saving action, "for God is at work in you, both to will and to work for his good pleasure" (Phil. 2:13). The Church is not independent from Christ, it is His body. Saint Paul learned this lesson powerfully on the road to Damascus. When knocked to the ground, he heard a voice saying, "Saul, Saul, why do you persecute *me*?" (Acts 9:4). Jesus did not say Saul was persecuting the Church, but that he was persecuting Him. Christ has identified Himself completely with the Church. We, as Christians, are to extend His saving work. Saint Paul teaches us clearly, "For we are God's fellow workers; you are God's field, God's building" (1 Cor. 3:9). Each of us is supposed to manifest Christ to the world. Mary is simply a Christian, the first and most perfect Christian.

Giving Glory to God

The teachings of Christ do not simply show us how to avoid hell and achieve heaven. They also allow us to make sense out of *this* life. In Christ, God has taken the broken, fractured family of humanity and restored it and made it anew as the Family of God. If we forsake this biblical teaching of family, we will fall away from God's plan and away from the Church, the Family of God.

In the beginning, God created us in His image and likeness. He created us male and female and told us to be fruitful and multiply. The family is a God-given model, or icon, for us to make sense out of this life and out of the life of God. Only when we forget this, do we find ourselves falling back into a spirit of competition according to which honoring Mary takes away from honoring God. Families do not speak this way. You will never hear me say, as a father, do not honor my son because it takes honor away from me. No, when you honor my son, you bring honor to me. So it is with God. Even more than the miracle of creation, the greatest work of God is our sanctification. When we honor the holiness, the goodness, and the love found in a human soul, we don't take away from the honor of God; we manifest it. This is most true of the Blessed Virgin Mary.

When we turn to the teachings about Mary with this biblical perspective, we find the clear teachings of historic apostolic Christianity. We begin to see that many of our objections are founded upon half-truths. Yes, Jesus Christ is the one mediator, but He exercises His mediation by imparting His Spirit to His saints. Each of us raises our prayers to heaven for one another, our brothers and sisters, and for those still waiting to find faith in Christ. This role of intercessor is especially true of His mother, who reigns as queen in the kingdom of God.

In the latter chapters of this book, we will examine Marian devotion, including the Rosary, and see that when Our Lord condemns vain repetition in Matthew 6:7, He is doing just that—condemning *vain* repetition. Our Lord Himself repeats His prayers. For example, in the Garden of Gethsemane we are told, "leaving them again, he went away and prayed for the third time, saying the same words" (Mt. 26:44). As blood was streaming from the face of Our Lord in the midst of His agony, no one could accuse His repetitious prayer of being vain or meaningless. In fact, Scripture teaches that in the heavenly liturgy, where we will worship God in spirit and truth, the angels and saints pray the same words over and over, "Holy, holy, holy":

> And the four living creatures, each of them with six wings, are full of eyes all round and within, and day and night they never cease to sing, "Holy, holy, holy, is the Lord God Almighty, who was and is and is to come!" (Rev. 4:8).

Certainly we would not accuse the angelic hosts of vain repetition simply because they repeat their words.

Image Isn't Everything

As we examine the teachings of Sacred Scripture within the context of apostolic and historic Christianity, we will recognize why the Church has always stood against those who would reject sacred images, which was condemned as the heresy of iconoclasm by the Second Council of Nicea in 787. Yes, the Ten Commandments clearly forbid the making of graven images, but this is not an absolute prohibition against the use of images in our worship.

An incident from the Old Testament proves this point. Almost immediately after Moses receives the Ten Commandments, he is instructed directly by God to build the tabernacle. God requires Moses to build the tabernacle according to a specific plan:

> And let them make me a sanctuary, that I may dwell in their midst. According to all that I show you concerning the pattern of the tabernacle, and of all its furniture, so you shall make it (Ex. 25:8-9).

The fact that Moses is following a pattern given to him by God is stressed again in Exodus 25:40 and 26:30. It is interesting to note that the pattern that Almighty God Himself gives to Moses requires him to make graven images of angels and to place them in the holiest of places in the Jewish religion:

> And you shall make two cherubim of gold; of hammered work shall you make them, on the two ends of the mercy seat. Make one cherub on the one end, and one cherub on the other end; of one piece with the mercy seat shall you make the cherubim on its two ends. The cherubim shall spread out their wings above, overshadowing the mercy seat with their wings, their faces one to another; toward the mercy seat shall the faces of the cherubim be (Ex. 25:18-20).

Therefore, even in the Old Testament we can see that sacred images are not absolutely condemned. Images are used to remind us of the supernatural realities that surround us. Even on a natural level we use photographs to remind us of our loved ones. When I look upon a picture of my wife and children, I am not tempted to be unfaithful to them, rather I am reminded of the love that I have for each of them. Nor do I confuse the image with the reality.

There is a subtle distinction that those who are opposed to graven images fail to make (cf. Heb. 5:8). It is always and everywhere wrong to worship graven images, but the consistent witness of both Judaism and Christianity shows that it is lawful to make use of sacred images in worshiping the true God. We use sacred images to draw our minds toward the heavenly realities. In icons, paintings, and statues, Mary is shown to be close to her Son. This closeness, illustrated in art, is the key to Mary's sanctity—and ours.

The New Eve

Mary's holiness is the work of her Son, because Mary alone among all women has a Son who existed before her. God the Son did not wait until He took flesh to bless His mother, but from the first moment of her conception, His saving work began within her soul. Those who reject the Immaculate Conception because it seems to raise Mary up to the level of a goddess in no need of salvation have missed the point. Mary is saved by her Son in a manner that uniquely manifests His divine power.

Not too long ago, we were visiting with some friends. We happened to be sitting near a swimming pool. As we spoke, our children were playing in the shallow end. All of a sudden my wife leaped to her feet, and fully clothed she jumped into the pool. Before I knew what was happening my wife had grabbed our son who had drifted too far into the deep end and was completely submerged. My wife had saved him. There are two ways to save someone from drowning: You can pull them out of the water or you can keep them from ever falling into it in the first place. Jesus saves us by pulling us out of the water of sin. He saved Mary by protecting her from ever falling in at all. In Mary, we see a fulfillment of Genesis 3:15. Because of Christ's salvation, Mary is ever at enmity with the devil and, unlike us, is never held hostage to sin and the power of the evil one.

The unbroken testimony of Christian history bears witness to the holiness of Mary. Her purity is prefigured throughout the Old Testament, just as Jesus is prefigured in numerous *events*—for example, the binding of Isaac by his father Abraham on Mount Moriah (the eventual site of the Jewish Temple, outside of which Jesus would later be bound and offered up)—and *people*. For example, Jesus is prefigured by Solomon, the son of King David the peacemaker, whose name literally means "shalom" or "peace." Solomon is the Temple builder, and he points towards the great fulfillment of the real Son of David, the true King of Israel, the real bringer of peace, and the builder of the new and everlasting Temple. So too, Mary the New Eve, is foreshadowed throughout the Scriptures, as we will see in the next chapter. When we read the Scriptures the way Christ would have read them, we understand Mary as the fulfillment of "the woman" who is present from Genesis to Revelation (Gen. 3:15; Jn. 2:4; 19:26; Rev. 12:17).

Sign of Contradiction

Mary is a model of the mystery of the Christian life. This humble handmaid of the Lord has been exalted as Queen of Heaven. This is the work of Christ and all Christians are called by God to rejoice in it (cf. Lk. 1:48). In this book, we hope to plunge deeply into Sacred Scripture and examine apostolic and historic Christianity to see why Christians have followed in Christ's footsteps in honoring His mother. Our response to Mary is intimately bound up in our response to her Son. Simeon the prophet, under the inspiration of the Holy Spirit, turned to Mary as she was with her Son in the Temple and said:

> Behold, this child is set for the fall and rising of many in Israel, and for a sign that is spoken against (and a sword will pierce through your own soul also), that thoughts out of many hearts may be revealed (Lk. 2:34-35).

In some way, our hearts are revealed in our response to Mary. The rest of this book will allow us to evaluate our response to the mother of Jesus, in light of the teachings of Scripture and the insights of historic Christianity. It is my prayer that you will see that each of us is called to be Catholic for a reason.

Curtis Martin is the founding president of the Fellowship Of Catholic University Students (FOCUS), a dynamic college campus evangelization and leadership training program. He received his bachelor's degree in communications from Louisiana State University and his master's degree in theology from Franciscan University of Steubenville. He resides in Greeley, Colorado, with his wife Michaelann and their six children.

CHAPTER III

The "Woman" in Salvation History
Reflections of Mary in the Old Testament

CURTIS MITCH

Returning to a full appreciation of the Catholic Church after a prolonged period of disinterest and skepticism brings many challenges. For me, these hurdles had everything to do with the interpretation of Sacred Scripture. In college I rediscovered the riches of the Church after much involvement with an interdenominational Christian group on campus. Helped along by prayer, study, and a handful of Bishop Sheen tapes, I slowly began to appreciate the Bible's Catholic treasures. The Eucharist started to make sense in light of Jesus' words at the Last Supper; the primacy and leadership of Peter seemed logical to me and substantiated by the Bible; the close connection between Baptism and salvation gradually presented itself as a central teaching of the apostles. The final obstacle that kept me from an unreserved commitment to the Church could be summed up in a question: How could Catholic Tradition make so much of Mary when the New Testament seems to say so little about her? In other words, could I accept the argument that the unique quality of biblical passages about Mary sufficiently compensates for the lack of quantity?

As far as I could tell at the time, there were no easy answers to questions regarding Mary's place in Scripture. Seeing a full-color, biblical portrait of Mary within the framework of the Church's teaching would involve a fuller study of Scripture than I was used to; lining up doctrinal proof-texts like beads on a string would simply not do. I later discovered that the Church's Tradition captured the whole truth about Mary by seeing her in the whole of God's revelation. The profound mystery and role of Jesus' mother thus revolved around the mystery of Scripture itself and God's overarching plan of salvation—a plan which embraces both Testaments, Old and New.

The Old Revealed in the New

Early on I learned that much of the Bible's teaching about Mary exists in the form of Old Testament types. This means, among other things, that direct prophecy was not the only way that the Old Testament announced the glorious advent of the New. In addition to prophetic oracles about the future Messiah and His mother (e.g., Gen. 3:15; Is. 7:14), God used various people, places, events, and institutions of the Old Covenant to prefigure the mysteries He would later unveil through Christ. As the Author of creation, God was not bound to speak to His people only with *words*; He also adapted created *things* for His purposes and invested them with spiritual and prophetic sig-nificance.[1] In biblical language, these historical preparations for the Gospel are called *types* (Gk. *typos*). This word was used by the New Testament writers to mean a "copy," "model," or "figure" and literally refers to a stamp or mark made when one object strikes another.[2] For example, an impression made in clay by a

---

[1] This classic teaching of the Church Fathers is summed up by Saint Thomas Aquinas (*Summa Theologiae* Ia q. 1, art. 10): "The author of Holy Writ is God, in whose power it is to signify His meaning, not by words only (as man also can do), but also by things themselves."

[2] For further details, see Ceslas Spicq, O.P., *Theological Lexicon of the New Testament*, vol. 3, trans. James D. Ernest (Peabody, MA: Hendrickson Publishers, 1994), 384-87.

signet ring or seal would leave a mark that resembled its crafted image, yet differed from it as a copy differs from an original. Old Covenant "types" thus referred to historical persons and things that pointed forward to greater realities yet to be revealed; they were prophetic impressions of Christianity stamped throughout the sacred history of ancient Israel. These reflections of the New Covenant in the Old Testament were part of what made the entire Bible a living source of the Church's teaching throughout the centuries.

In general, typology bridges the distance and solidifies the relationship between the Old and the New Testaments. Viewed broadly, it means that God's worldwide plan of salvation, reaching across many centuries, is unified and continuous; the numerous stories and events of the Bible are various subplots that contribute to the larger story of redemption that finally unfolds in Christ. The New Testament must not be viewed as a new book, but as the final and climactic chapter of biblical history. It is the continuation of everything that preceded it and the full blossoming of all that was foretold and foreshadowed in the Old Testament. We see in the Gospels, for instance, how Jesus looked to the Jerusalem Temple, the experience of Jonah, and King Solomon as historical prototypes of Himself and His ministry (Mt. 12:6, 41-42). God positioned these key persons and places to face forward and point beyond themselves toward something greater yet to come. Saint Paul likewise interprets the Gospel in light of its preparatory stages in the Old Testament, calling the first man Adam a "type" of the greater Person of Jesus (cf. Rom. 5:14). By way of contrast, Adam's disastrous rebellion was outmatched by the glorious redemption of Christ (cf. Rom. 5:15). Saint Peter similarly saw events of the biblical past in terms of the present, perceiving in the ancient flood an advance presentation of Baptism which more perfectly cleanses away the sin and filth of the world (1 Pet. 3:21).

Since the surpassing glory of the New Covenant was part of a long process of preparation and education for Israel, it was only reasonable for the evangelists and the early Fathers of the Church to search the Scriptures looking for images of Mary. After all, she played an outstanding role in bearing and nurturing God's Son precisely when biblical history reached its crowning moment (cf. Gal. 4:4). She was uniquely privileged to stand at the doorway between the old and the new—the threshold of sacred time when promises gave way to fulfillment and the shadowy "types" dissipated to reveal the glorious vessel they were meant to prefigure.

A Treasury of Marian Types

Catholic Tradition has culled numerous Marian gems from the rich mines of the Old Testament (cf. Catechism, no. 489). Many such "types" of Mary are linked with the sacred, albeit impersonal, objects which stand out in the Scriptures for their central and memorable role in Israel's history. Pope Pius IX, when defining the Immaculate Conception, gave a brief index of Marian typology that figured prominently in the writings of the Fathers and the ancient liturgical prayers of the Church.[3] *Noah's ark* (Gen. 7:7), for instance, prefigured Mary's singular purity and immunity from sin, for it alone escaped the dreadful judgment of God upon the world for its wickedness. *Jacob's ladder* (Gen. 28:12) typified the Blessed Virgin as a heavenly intercessor, stretching up to the Lord and serving as the avenue whereupon angels and blessings pass between heaven and earth. The *burning bush* (Ex. 3:2) is a type of Mary as a mother enveloped in divine love—just as the bush burned but was not consumed, so the Virgin remained uncharred by the raging flames of God's presence in her womb. *Solomon's Temple* (1 Kings 8:10-13) likewise foreshadows the mystery of her divine maternity: As God's glory filled the sacred building, so Mary became a sanctuary housing the glory of God's Son. The Litany of Loreto similarly

---

[3] Pope Pius IX, Apostolic Constitution Defining the Dogma of the Immaculate Conception *Ineffabilis Deus* (1854), (Boston: St. Paul Books & Media), 13-14.

addresses Mary as the *Ark of the Covenant*.[4] Just as the golden ark held within it such things as the tablets of the law and a sample of heavenly manna, so Mary bore within her womb Jesus Christ, the living law of the New Covenant and the Eucharistic Bread of Life.

In addition to the symbolism of inanimate objects, Mary is also typified by the women and mothers of the Old Covenant.[5] These outstanding figures exhibit a real but limited likeness to the mother of the future Messiah and prepared Israel to welcome her as their most exemplary and virtuous kinswoman. Foremost among these ancient women is *Eve*, the mother of all the living (Gen. 3:20). The Church Fathers, following the same trajectory that Saint Paul traced when contrasting Adam with Jesus (cf. Rom. 5:14; 1 Cor. 15:22), likewise defined Mary's antithetical relationship to Eve. Mary stands as the blessed counterpart to Eve. Unlike the first woman, the Virgin always obeyed God, was always at enmity with the treacherous serpent, and was made the mother of all who are spiritually alive through grace.[6]

Rebekah prefigured Mary in her maternal concern to secure blessings for her son Jacob and shield him from the plots of his envious brother Esau (Gen. 25-27). Like this matriarch, the Blessed Mother protects her children from the tactics of the enemy, gives them wise counsel, and petitions the Father to bless them.[7]

The *mother of the Maccabean martyrs* (2 Mac. 7) is a striking prototype of Mary in her maternal anguish. She encouraged her sons to trust unswervingly in God despite torture, convinced that

---

[4] See chapter five. A printed edition of the Litany may be found in Rev. James D. Watkins, *Manual of Prayers* Pontifical North American College Rome (Huntington, IN: Our Sunday Visitor, 1998), 2nd ed., 117-20.

[5] For a helpful summary of these women in relation to Mary, see Stefano M. Manelli, F.F.I., *All Generations Shall Call Me Blessed*, trans. Peter Damian Fehlner, F.F.I. (New Bedford, MA: Academy of the Immaculate, 1995), 50-58.

[6] See chapter four.

[7] For more extensive parallels, see Saint Louis De Montfort, *True Devotion to Mary*, trans. Fr. Fredrick Faber (Rockford, IL: TAN Books & Publishers, 1985), 116-34.

God would vindicate her sons and raise them again from the dead. Echoes of this event can be heard in the background as Mary stood at the foot of the Cross, pained at the spectacle of her tortured Son, yet full of motherly confidence in the divine promise of resurrection.[8]

Precedents for the royal dignity of Mary can be traced to the prominent queens of the Old Testament era.[9] *Queen Esther* (Esther 1-10) was a remarkable heroine whose advantaged position in the Persian kingdom enabled her to avert a planned massacre of her fellow Jews in exile. Mary similarly uses her heavenly authority and intervention as Queen to protect God's people from the deadly schemes of the devil. *Queen Bathsheba* was known as a powerful intercessor exercising great maternal sway over her son, King Solomon (1 Kings 2:13-25). Her royal advocacy in the kingdom of Israel speaks prophetic volumes about Mary's greater and more effective intercession before Christ, the true successor and Son of David enthroned in heaven (cf. Mk. 16:19; Lk. 1:32).

We might ask ourselves, with some justification, whether these Marian types found in the Old Testament are instances of mere fanciful creativity, or examples that are firmly anchored in the inspired text of Scripture. That is, how do we know that Marian types are *in* the Bible and not just in the minds of its interpreters? We will better understand the Church's interpretive tradition when we examine how the New Testament itself confirms Marian typology and gives the Church an advantaged angle for seeing the Virgin throughout biblical history. It will be helpful, therefore, to enter into this tradition for ourselves; like the artistry of stained-glass windows, the subtle colors and contours of Marian typology can hardly be appreciated unless they are viewed from the inside. Since Old Testament portraits of Mary often take their cue from the revealed words of the

---

[8] See Eric May, O.F.M. Cap., "Mary in the Old Testament," in Juniper B. Carol, O.F.M., ed., *Mariology* (Milwaukee: The Bruce Publishing Company, 1955), vol. 1, 75.

[9] See chapter six.

New, this will be the best place to examine in greater detail one of the more intriguing examples of Marian typology grounded in Scripture.

Blessed Among Women

The first two chapters of Luke's Gospel are widely cherished among Bible readers. They narrate the stories of John the Baptist's conception and birth, the Annunciation to Mary and, of course, the Nativity and early childhood of Jesus. Situated in the midst of these profound events, however, is the humble occasion of Mary's Visitation to Elizabeth (Lk. 1:39-56). On the surface, the episode appears dwarfed and overshadowed by the towering mysteries which surround it; nevertheless, it too is a mystery of the Rosary and has a spiritual significance all its own—a significance in part derived from its connections with the Old Testament.

The storyline is a simple and familiar one: Mary heard from the angel Gabriel that her kinswoman Elizabeth—despite old age and a long history of barrenness—had conceived a child and was now six months pregnant. Overjoyed at the news, Mary set out "with haste" (Lk. 1:39) to visit her cousin by taking a long trek from Nazareth to the hill country of Judah. Nothing extraordinary seemed to characterize these events until the two women finally met. All of a sudden, the Holy Spirit descended mightily on Elizabeth, the infant John jostled with joy in her womb, and she burst out in one of the most exuberant cries in Scripture: "Blessed are you among women, and blessed is the fruit of your womb!" (Lk. 1:42). Were it not for the nudging impulse of the Spirit, we might have thought Mary's cousin was overstating things a bit. How could Elizabeth have already known that Mary was chosen to be the mother of the Messiah? How could she (and John!) have a clear picture of the mystery within her before Christ was revealed to the world? It had to be the Holy Spirit who illumined her mind and moved her soul in this way; only divine light could reveal that this maiden and her infant were the most blessed mother and child in history.

But what did the words "Blessed are you among women" really mean? For the Catholic reader, this expression immediately recalls the beloved prayer, the "Hail Mary." For Elizabeth and Mary, however, these words were strikingly similar to certain appellations in the Old Testament.

The first time a statement like this found expression in the Bible was centuries earlier in the Book of Judges. The story is told of a heroine named Jael who stands out as one of the most valiant women in Old Testament history (Judg. 4-5). She lived at a time when the people of Israel were like wandering sheep, with shepherds (i.e., judges) rising up only sporadically to give them spiritual guidance. Plagued by unstable leadership and deficient faith, God's people were caught in a vicious cycle of sin and repentance that repeatedly called down God's judgment upon them. In Jael's day, the Canaanites were God's chosen form of discipline for His wayward people. They pressed heavily upon Israel and treated them cruelly for many years; their military commander, Sisera, was particularly vicious and feared. When at last the Lord came to Israel's assistance, He orchestrated a great battle through the prophetess Deborah and gave Israel a smashing victory over their oppressors. Every Canaanite warrior fell on the battlefield that fateful day except one—Sisera.

The Canaanite commander fled the scene in an attempt to save his life. He eventually came to lodge in the tent of Jael, thinking it a safe haven for military strategists on Israel's "Most Wanted" list. He was sadly mistaken. Jael turned the tables on the mighty Sisera without his even realizing it: She crept stealthily to his bedside, drove a tent peg through his skull, and fashioned his head rather crudely to the floor of her tent! (Judg. 4:21). Though a humble woman without any known expertise in the art of war, she single-handedly brought low the chief enemy of God's people. For this reason Deborah hailed her with the exalted words: "Most blessed of women be Jael . . . of tent-dwelling women most blessed" (Judg. 5:24). This is the first biblical echo that whispers—if not shouts—behind the words of Elizabeth in Luke 1:42.

Valiant Warrior

The Book of Judith furnishes us with a second. Like Jael, Judith stands out in the Old Testament as a woman of unforgettable courage. She too lived during turbulent times in Israel's history when the ambitions of foreign empires posed a constant threat to God's people. As the story goes, Judith was a woman of renowned piety and stunning beauty. She assumed center stage when the armies of Nebuchadnezzar, led by the general Holofernes, embarked on a series of military campaigns throughout the region, coming into the very heartland of Israel. Judith's hometown of Bethulia was the first stop on Holofernes' list. Here he breathed arrogant threats against the inhabitants and seized the city's water supply in hopes of starving them into submission. With circumstances growing more desperate every day, Judith prayed fervently to the Lord and began to devise a strategy for victory.

Judith's plan involved leaving the city and presenting herself to Holofernes as a defector from Israel and a useful informant. So with serpent-like wisdom and dove-like innocence she presented herself to the general as an attractive woman seeking refuge from the war. Her beauty captivated Holofernes, while her ulterior designs remained undetected. One night after feasting and drinking heavily, Holofernes found himself alone with Judith in his tent. Overcome with wine, however, he fell quickly into a deep sleep. Judith wasted no time in seizing the moment. Holofernes had unwittingly positioned himself in checkmate as the courageous woman took the general's own sword and cut off his head! Quickly she slipped out of the tent with the ghastly trophy of the commander's head tucked in a bag and returned to the beleaguered city. All rejoiced that the Lord wrought such an astonishing victory for Israel through the humble maiden Judith. The episode reached a climax when the city magistrate Uzziah came to her exclaiming: "O daughter, you are blessed by the Most High God above all women on earth" (Jud. 13:18). In the end, Judith's performance proved to be a turning point in

Israel's history; like Jael, she was a "blessed" vessel chosen by God to crush the stronghold of the enemy.

With this background now in the forefront of our minds, it is nearly impossible to imagine that Elizabeth could have spoken such words as "Blessed are you among women" without triggering a flood of biblical associations. Indeed the Spirit Himself—the same Holy Spirit who inspired the Scriptures— must have chosen such words for this very purpose. We can now see Mary standing in a long tradition of valiant biblical women whom God selected to carry forward His saving plan. Jael and Judith played such pivotal roles in the Old Testament as types that they prefigured the mission of the Messiah's mother.

Beyond general points of correspondence, the common denominator linking together the experiences of Jael and Judith is the violent downfall of God's adversaries. Both women were chosen to strike down the commanding officer of enemy forces with a lethal blow to the head. The question that immediately presents itself to us is obvious: What possible connections could such brutal details have with the quiet life of Mary? In what specific way was she really like these biblical heroines?

Questions like these inevitably push the attentive reader into the historical context of ancient Judaism, a world with magnificent hopes for the coming Messiah. Like any and every Jew, Elizabeth would have known many ancient prophecies foretelling the advent of Israel's deliverer. Doubtless, then, she knew well the very first prophecy of the Old Testament: "I will put enmity between you and the woman, and between your seed and her seed; he shall bruise your head, and you shall bruise his heel" (Gen. 3:15). With this promise, God announced far in advance of its fulfillment that the devil's triumph in the Garden of Eden would eventually end in defeat, with his head being crushed or bruised under the trampling blows of the Messiah and His mother.

We can safely say that Jews would not be prone to forget such bright promises so graphically depicted. Elizabeth was no exception. In a flash of inspired intuition, this ancient prophesy

(Gen. 3:15) converged with the ancient types of Jael and Judith in the mind of Elizabeth, yielding a biblical portrait of the maiden standing before her. She realized that this humble, expectant mother was to play a leading role with her Son in the great drama of redemption. Thus while Mary's blessedness was prefigured in the lives of Israel's valiant women, the comparisons worked out to her advantage—for both the enemy fought (Satan) and the victory won (over sin) would be immeasurably greater. This Mary was at one level the mirror image of women like Jael, Judith, and other memorable heroines; at another, she stood far above them as the most exemplary woman in history.[10] Stunned by the impact of this mystery, Elizabeth could do nothing but clothe her thoughts in the poignant words of Scripture: "Blessed are you among women" (Lk. 1:42). She must have felt deeply privileged that afternoon to announce that the feminine "types" of the Old Covenant had now seen their fulfillment in this young mother who had come for a visit.

The Mystery of Mary

The role of Mary in Sacred Scripture can seem like both a puzzle and a hurdle—for practicing Catholics, non-Catholics, and returning Catholics alike. Guided by the Church's Tradition, however, we can be led from the surface of the Bible into the depths of its Old and New Testament teaching about the Blessed Mother. This chapter has outlined something of how God's care-

---

[10] It is unfortunate that popular Protestant apologists sometimes take Elizabeth's words "Blessed are you among women" to mean that Mary was only one among many great women and in no way elevated above them. This falters on two accounts: (1) The importance and dignity of Mary's motherhood is derived from the greatness of her Son. No one should question that Mary was blessed in a way that was unlike other women; only one vessel, after all, could be the chosen mother of the divine Messiah. (2) Elizabeth's expression reflects a Semitic way of speaking, where positive statements are often used in the Bible with a comparative or superlative meaning (cf. Song. 1:8 LXX). In this case, her words would be better rendered, "Most blessed are you among women." For details, see Maximilian Zerwick, S.J., *Biblical Greek*, trans. Joseph Smith, S.J. (Rome: *Scripta Pontificii Instituti Biblici*, 1963), no. 146.

ful crafting of ancient Marian types had as its purpose to fix in the minds of His people images of the most perfect woman still to come. The mystery of Mary was thus something long prepared for and something that ultimately surpassed even the grandest expectations of Israel. Little wonder that when she arrived in her immaculate glory, Christians would thereafter see in the ancient Scriptures so many hints and prophetic reflections of the woman they affectionately called "Mother." Only Saint Paul could get away with compressing such cardinal mysteries of the New Covenant into a single, brief statement: "But when the time had fully come, God sent forth his Son, born of woman" (Gal. 4:4).

Curtis Mitch received his master's degree in theology from Franciscan University of Steubenville. He formerly worked as a lay pastoral associate in the Diocese of Pittsburgh, Pennsylvania, and is currently working on a Catholic study Bible that will be published by Ignatius Press. He resides in Steubenville, Ohio, with his wife Stacy and their three children.

CHAPTER IV

Mary as
the New Eve

TIM GRAY

History, according to the vision of the Catholic Church, is the story of God's relationship to man, "His story," otherwise known as salvation history. But salvation history is history. It is the dramatic story of God's reaching out to His people, restoring the rebellious family of Adam (humanity) into the Trinitarian Family of God. The climax of history comes when God the Father sends His own Son into the midst of history, for the salvation of the world. According to Saint Paul, "when the time had fully come, God sent forth his Son, born of woman" (Gal. 4:4).

Mary is the means by which Jesus comes into the story, into history. Mary's motherhood marks the fullness of time, the maturity of the Father's plan for salvation. It is Mary's motherhood that defines her role, the part that God has chosen for her to play in the drama of salvation history. This role not only comes at the fullness of time, but transforms all time. Mary's role is so central to the story that it is foreshadowed in the past and continues in the present and future.

At the outset of the Bible's story, the virgin Eve is approached by the devil, who appears in the form of a serpent. Eve lets her trust in the Creator die in her heart and disobeys the divine command not to eat of the fruit of the forbidden tree that stands in the midst of paradise. Eve's defiant act of independence will lead her, and the entire human family, into subjection to Satan and wretched servitude to sin. Starting with Eve and then her husband Adam, sin came into the world through the message of a fallen angel. But this terrible beginning will be overcome by the message of another angel, one who stands before the throne of the Holy One.

In the fullness of time, Gabriel is sent to a young virgin named Mary. Mary receives the angel's word with faith and, through her obedience, the solution to Eve's ancient problem of disobedience and death is conceived, for in her is Jesus. Mary, the model of humility, affirms her complete dependence upon God and utters her *fiat* ("let it be done"). What is the meaning of the striking contrast between these two women? The answer is that in Mary, God is solving the problem of sin that entered the world through Eve. Scripture takes up this drama in Revelation 12.

Sparing the Rod?

John's dazzling vision of heaven in chapter twelve of Revelation reveals a "woman clothed with the sun, with the moon under her feet, and on her head a crown of twelve stars" (Rev. 12:1). Then another astounding sight appears in the heavens, "a great red dragon, with seven heads and ten horns, and seven diadems upon his heads" (12:3). The chapter goes on to describe the ensuing war between the woman and the dragon, between the woman's offspring and the dragon's evil minions. But who are the "woman" and the dragon, and what is this cosmic conflict all about?

We know the woman by the fruit she bears. She gives birth to a male child, one who is "to rule *all the nations with a rod of iron*" (Rev. 12:5). For those who have ears to hear, this description clearly discloses the child's identity. This is a direct allusion to Psalm 2, where the Lord tells the promised Messiah that He will rule all the nations:

> Ask of me, and I will make *the nations your heritage*, and the ends of the earth your possession. You shall break them with a *rod of iron*, and dash them in pieces like a potter's vessel (Ps. 2:8-9).

Undoubtedly the woman's child is the long-awaited Messiah. Since Jesus is the Messiah, the woman is none other than Mary.

But if the woman is Mary, the mother of Jesus, why does John simply refer to her as the "woman"? We could ask this same question regarding John's reference to the child simply as the "one who is to rule all the nations with a rod of iron" (Rev. 12:5). Rather than giving us Jesus' name, John employs the rich symbolic language of Israel's prophetic tradition. This symbolism is not esoteric or confusing. Rather, it imbues John's description of the events of salvation history with their rich theological significance. Only the deeply symbolic language of Scripture can do justice to the profound meaning wrapped in the events of salvation history. Just as the description of the child "subduing the nations with an iron rod" draws on salvation history to reveal Jesus as the long-awaited Messiah, so the theological significance of the title "woman" is revealed by its allusion to an earlier biblical prophecy.

The Prophetic Woman

By calling Mary "woman," John echoes an important prophecy of the Old Testament—the very first prophecy ever made! In the third chapter of Genesis, immediately after the fall of Adam and Eve, God curses the serpent saying, "I will put enmity between you and *the woman*, and between your seed and her seed" (Gen. 3:15), thus foretelling the perpetual conflict between the forces of Satan and the descendants of the woman. The Lord continues speaking to the serpent, declaring that the

woman and her seed would conquer the serpent: "he shall
bruise your head, and you shall bruise his heel" (*ibid.*). This
last line can be a bit confusing, but once it is remembered that
the "you" is the serpent, it becomes clear that the "he" who
strikes the serpent's head is the male seed of the woman. The
serpent in turn can only strike at his heel, thereby signifying the
ultimate victory of the woman's seed over the devil. Christian
tradition has always seen this passage as the first prophetic
promise that a messiah would arise and defeat the demonic
enemy. This prophecy has been called the *proto-evangelium*.
This Latin phrase means the "first gospel," the first announcement of the Good News.

Thus Scripture begins by describing the drama of salvation history as the struggle between the serpent and the woman, between
his evil followers (human and angelic) and her descendants. Is John
comparing the woman of Genesis 3 (Eve) with the woman of
Revelation 12 (Mary)? Yes. His comparison becomes even more
obvious once a few of the similarities between Genesis 3 and
Revelation 12 are brought into sharp focus.

In addition to God, there are three main protagonists in
Genesis 3: the serpent, Adam, and the woman. In Revelation
12, there are also three main protagonists: the dragon (who in
Revelation 12:9 is identified as "that *ancient serpent*, who is
called the Devil and Satan, the deceiver of the whole world"),
the messianic child, Jesus (who is the "new Adam" [cf. Rom.
5:14; 1 Cor. 15:45]), and the woman. The correspondence is
striking. Other details linking the two scenes are the conflict
between the woman and the ancient serpent, and the pain of
childbirth for both women (Gen. 3:16; Rev. 12:2). John's
point is that Mary is "the woman" and that her seed, Jesus,
brings about the defeat of the ancient serpent. For John, there
is no better way to describe world-shattering events, such as
the fulfillment of the *proto-evangelium* and the identification
of the long-awaited "woman" and her messianic offspring,
than with the theologically rich symbolic language of Israel's
prophetic tradition.

Full of Grace

Saint John gives Mary the title "woman" in order to show us that Mary is the *New Eve*, the woman whose child would defeat the dreaded dragon. Pope John Paul II observes that, "From this vantage point the two female figures *Eve* and *Mary* are joined under the *name of woman*."[1] As early as the second century, the Church Fathers concluded that since Jesus is the "New Adam," Mary is the New Eve.[2] Saint Irenaeus said, "[T]he knot of Eve's disobedience was untied by Mary's obedience: what the virgin Eve had bound through her disbelief, Mary loosened by her faith."[3] It is worth noting that Saint Irenaeus was a disciple of Saint Polycarp who was a disciple of Saint John, the beloved disciple. Thus this patristic teaching of Mary as the New Eve goes straight back to Saint John himself. Mary is the true Eve, the true "mother of the living" (cf. Gen. 3:20).

Eve is the biological mother of us all, but Mary's spiritual maternity surpasses Eve's physical maternity. Eve's glory is eclipsed by her disobedience, whereas Mary's glory rests on her obedience. One is the mother of our fallen nature, the other is the mother full of grace. Eve comes at the beginning of creation, and her fall, along with Adam's, sets the tragic trajectory of the Old Covenant. Mary comes at the dawn of the new era, described by Isaiah as the new heavens and new earth (cf. Is. 65:17), and her obedience along with the New Adam's sets the triumphant trajectory of the New Covenant. Thus the ancient motto attributed to Saint Jerome, "death through Eve, life through Mary."[4]

In the contrast made between the old and New Eve, it must be noted that Mary's faith and obedience are the cause of her fame.

---

[1] Pope John Paul II, Apostolic Letter On the Dignity and Vocation of Women *Mulieris Dignitatem* (1988), no. 11, original emphasis.

[2] Saint Justin Martyr (d.c. 165) compares Mary to Eve in his *Dialogue with Trypho*, 100, as translated in *Ante-Nicene Fathers*, vol. I, A. Roberts and J. Donaldson, eds., (Peabody, MA: Hendrickson Publishers, 1994), 249.

[3] Saint Irenaeus, *Adversus Haereses* (*Against Heresies*), 3, 22, 4, as quoted in LG 56.

[4] As quoted in LG 56. Already by the time of Saint Jerome this idea has taken the form of a slogan.

Mary is primarily honored for her faith, a faithful obedience through which she became the Mother of the Word. Thus Tertullian observes that the most striking contrast between Mary and Eve is in the matter of faith: "As Eve had believed the serpent, so Mary believed the angel [Gabriel]. The delinquency which the one occasioned by believing, the other by believing effaced."[5] This perspective is important, as is demonstrated in the biblical passage often wrongly used to downplay the significance of Mary. Some who misunderstand or are hostile to the honor paid to Mary cite the following passage as evidence that the role of Mary's motherhood of God is inconsequential to the plan of salvation.

> While he was still speaking to the people, behold, his mother and his brethren stood outside, asking to speak to him. But he replied to the man who told him, "Who is my mother, and who are my brethren?" And stretching out his hand toward his disciples, he said, "Here are my mother and my brethren! For whoever does the will of my Father in heaven is my brother, and sister, and mother" (Mt. 12:46, 48-50).

Some argue that Jesus is minimizing family blood ties (including motherhood) in favor of the call to obedience to the Father's will. Family blood ties, including the mother-child relation, are almost trivial when compared to following Jesus and doing the Father's will. While this is true, the conclusion that Mary is therefore insignificant or no greater than any other disciple of Christ is unwarranted and mistaken. That merit is measured not by blood but by obedience to the Father, far from invalidating Mary's merit, affirms it. Mary fulfilled the will of the Father perfectly in her life. Her *fiat* echoes this: "Behold, I am the handmaid of the Lord; let it be to me according to your word" (Lk. 1:38). Elizabeth testifies to this when she greets Mary and says, "blessed

---

[5] Tertullian, *On the Flesh of Christ*, ch. 17, as translated in Alexander Roberts, D.D., and James Donaldson, LL.D., eds., *Ante-Nicene Fathers*, vol. 3 (Peabody, MA: Hendrickson Publishers, Inc., 1994), 536.

is she who believed that there would be a fulfillment of what was spoken to her from the Lord" (Lk. 1:45). If Noah, Abraham, David, and many others were chosen to serve God in special ways because of their righteousness, is it not ridiculous to think that God chose His mother at random? Surely Gabriel makes this evident when he greets Mary as "full of grace" and then tells her that he was sent because she has "found favor with God" (Lk. 1:28, 30).

It must also be remembered that Jesus said many things that seemed to downplay family ties. But Jesus was not anti-family. He was loosening the natural family blood ties to incorporate people into the true and ultimate family, His Father's family. Next to the Family of God, all other natural family bonds are less significant. This is illustrated by the following incident:

> Another of the disciples said to him, "Lord, let me first go and bury my father." But Jesus said to him, "Follow me, and leave the dead to bury their own dead" (Mt. 8:21-22).

Behind this seemingly outrageous command of Jesus is a radical transformation of true family commitments. "The only explanation for Jesus' astonishing command is that he envisioned loyalty to himself and his kingdom-movement as creating an alternative family."[6] Jesus was tearing down in order to build up. The old family of Adam was being reconstituted into the family of Christ. Far from being left behind in this new family, Mary is to be found at its forefront.

It is through Baptism and the Eucharist that Jesus establishes His New Covenant family. In Baptism we are spiritually born into the Family of God, and through the Eucharist we partake of the body and blood of Jesus, whereby all the faithful share the same blood—which makes Christian brotherhood a true kinship bond in the blood of Christ (cf. 1 Cor. 10:16). Since Jesus took His

---

[6] N.T. Wright, *Jesus and the Victory of God* (Minneapolis: Fortress Press, 1997), 401.

flesh and blood from the Virgin Mary, we who partake of the divine mysteries share a blood tie with Mary. Thus we are truly her children. If we take Jesus as our Brother, then we must have Mary as our mother.

Mother of the Church

One of the very last acts of Our Lord was His giving His mother Mary to us as our Mother.

> When Jesus saw his mother, and the disciple whom he loved standing near, he said to his mother, "Woman, behold, your son!" Then he said to the disciple, "Behold, your mother!" (Jn. 19:26-27).

The Church's tradition has always understood this passage to mean that Mary was given to all of Christ's disciples, those whom He loves, and that Mary is therefore the Mother of all Christians.

Some Christians have tried to argue against this view. They assert that Jesus is only entrusting Mary to John's protection and care because He is dying. Undoubtedly, Jesus is entrusting Mary into John's care, and vice versa. (It is worth noting that this incident confirms the early Fathers' view that Mary did not have any other children, since Jesus could not have entrusted Mary into the care of John if Jesus had other siblings, because the duty would have fallen on them.)

There is, however, a strong case for showing that more is going on than the conscientious care of a widow. First, Jesus was a prophet, and prophets were known for making symbolic actions. "Isaiah's nakedness, Jeremiah's smashed pot, and Ezekiel's brick come to mind as obvious examples,"[7] as do John the Baptist's living in the wilderness, sparse dress, and baptizing in the Jordan. Jesus followed this prophetic tradition in many ways, such as in turning over the money-changers' tables, cursing

---

[7] *Ibid.*, 415.

the barren fig tree (both of which symbolize the forthcoming destruction of the Temple), and choosing twelve apostles.

In light of these incidents, we must be prepared to see that Jesus' handing over of His mother to His beloved disciple would have symbolic import. In fact, one must wonder why, in recording the greatest event in history, John included his acquiring a new relationship to Mary, unless he knew that it had significance for the readers of his Gospel. John's careful description of the Passion of Our Lord puts great significance on every detail. If Jesus' action was not meant to be symbolic, why did the sacred author not use Mary's and John's names? The title "woman," as we have already seen, has strong prophetic connotations. Jesus' action makes sense when understood as the symbolic-prophetic sign that Mary is the Mother of all Christians. Mary becomes the spiritual mother of the Body of Christ (the Church) at the Cross. This is clearly how John interprets Jesus' intention, because in the last verse in chapter twelve of Revelation, John explicitly states who Mary's children are:

> Then the dragon was angry with the *woman*, and went off to make war on the *rest of her offspring*, on those who keep the commandments of God and bear testimony to Jesus (Rev. 12:17).

John is the only one of the twelve who follows Christ all the way to Calvary. Could it be accidental that the disciple closest to Mary was the one who had the courage to stand under the Cross? John was the first to take Mary as his spiritual mother. John therefore stands as a witness and sign that the fruit of Marian devotion is a love for Christ that is as strong as death. John shows that the disciple who takes Mary by the hand is able to follow Our Lord all the way to Calvary. As the Body of Christ goes through its corporate crucifixion (cf. Col. 1:24), one may well wonder whether the only disciples who will not flee in cowardice will be those who, like John, are children of Mary. We must beseech Mary that she will inflame our hearts with the same love and courage that John had on Good Friday.

We ceaselessly recall that nothing must ever make us forget the
reality and the consciousness that we are, all of us, sons of the
same Mother Mary, who lives in heaven, who is the bond of
union for the Mystical Body of Christ, and who as the [N]ew
Eve, and the new Mother of the living, desires to lead all men
to the truth and the grace of her divine Son.[8]

*Tim Gray is assistant professor of Scripture and catechetics at
the Notre Dame Graduate School of Christendom College in
Front Royal and Alexandria, Virginia. He is also the author of*
Mission of the Messiah *(Emmaus Road Publishing, 1999), a study
of St. Luke's Gospel. He resides in Castleton, Virginia, with his
wife Kris and their son Joseph.*

---

[8] Pope Pius XII, Address, "Fruits of the Definition," (November 1, 1950), as reprinted in
Benedictine Monks of Solemnes, *Papal Teachings: Our Lady*, Daughters of St. Paul,
trans. (Boston: Daughters of St. Paul, 1961), 323.

CHAPTER V

Mary, the God-bearing Ark

TIM GRAY

The light of the Son of God is so brilliant that it reaches throughout history, even into the far corners of the Old Testament. Just as the sun's light is reflected by the moon, so too, where the light of the Son of God shines, that light will be reflected by Mary. In keeping with Catholic tradition, Saint Pius X taught that where Christ is prefigured in the Old Testament, Mary was usually prefigured as well: "In a word, after Christ, we find in Mary the end of the law and the fulfillment of the figures and prophecies."[1] One example of this is the ark of the covenant, which bore the presence of God and thus foreshadowed Mary's bearing of Christ as the *Theotokos*, or Mother of God.

In the Old Covenant, God's presence or glory had dwelt in the tabernacle according to the instructions given to Moses. But access to God's tabernacle was prohibited, with the exception of the high priest, who could approach it only on the day of

---

[1] Pope Pius X, Encyclical Letter On the Immaculate Conception *Ad Diem Illum* (1904), no. 6; cf. LG 55.

atonement, after many sin offerings. Because of Israel's sin, the tabernacle was lost and God's concrete dwelling among His people was taken away in the exile, which continued up to Jesus' day. But with Mary's *fiat* at the Annunciation, God reestablished, in a greater and more intimate way, His dwelling among Israel. Rather than dwelling in a tabernacle made of gold and lined with precious gems, God made His dwelling within the flesh and blood of a human person, Mary. She is the ultimate tabernacle, gilded not by gold but by the grace of God. She is adorned not with gems but with the virtues, particularly humility and love. The Catechism notes that, in Mary, God the Father finally finds a proper dwelling place among men for His presence:

> For the first time in the plan of salvation and because his Spirit had prepared her, the Father found the *dwelling place* where his Son and his Spirit could dwell among men (no. 721, original emphasis).

Since Eden, God has desired to dwell among His people, and now "[i]n Mary, the Holy Spirit *fulfills* the plan of the Father's loving goodness" (Catechism, no. 723, original emphasis).

Precious Cargo

In the Old Testament, the ark of the covenant held three things: (1) the stone tablets upon which the finger of God had written the Ten Commandments on Mount Sinai, (2) a jar containing some of the manna which God had miraculously provided as food for the Israelites during their forty years in the desert, and (3) the staff of Aaron, the first high priest of the old law. The ark of the covenant was holy because of what was held inside of it, and its presence became synonymous with the presence of God among the Israelites. Where the ark of the covenant was, there also was the presence of Yahweh. Thus this holy vessel of God's presence was made and handled with special care. The latter chapters of Exodus tell us that the ark was hand-carved of acacia

wood and overlaid with pure gold, both within and without.
Only the Levites, the tribe which had been set aside for service of
the tabernacle, were supposed to carry the ark, and then only
with poles, themselves being overlaid with gold, that were fed
through rings of gold attached to the sides of the ark.

If in the Old Testament cult the ark, which was simply made
of precious gold and wood, held such a place of honor because it
mediated the presence of God, it is not surprising that Mary
holds a place of surpassing honor in the New Testament cult. The
ark bore the presence of God, and after the Annunciation Mary
bears God in her womb. Just as the ark contained the tablets of
the old law, the manna, and the staff of Aaron, Mary holds in her
womb Jesus Christ the Messiah, who is the new law, the living
bread from heaven, and the true high priest who offers His own
life for us.

That the early Christians understood Mary as the new ark of
the covenant is evident in Saint Luke's crafting of his account of
the Visitation (Lk. 1:39-56). Luke subtly parallels Mary's carrying
Jesus (in her womb) to visit Elizabeth with the ark's bearing the
presence of God to Jerusalem. In 2 Samuel 6 we hear how David,
aware of both his unworthiness that the ark should come to him
(v. 9) and of the immeasurable blessing that the presence of the
ark brings (v. 12), goes to bring the ark of the covenant up to
Jerusalem. David offers sacrifices (v. 13) and leaps and dances
(v. 16) before the ark as the procession progresses to Jerusalem
amid shouting and the sound of the horn (v. 15).

Saint Luke parallels his account of the Visitation with this
scene in 2 Samuel 6 to demonstrate that Mary is the new ark of
the covenant. Mary, like David, heads to the hill country of
Judah. As Mary, bearing Christ in her womb, approaches the
home of Elizabeth, Saint John the Baptist "leaps" in Elizabeth's
womb and she exclaims with a "loud cry," reminding us of
David's leaping before the ark of the covenant and the shouts of
the people of Israel. Elizabeth greets Mary with words similar to
those of David, "And why is this granted me, that the mother of
my Lord [who is the new ark of the covenant] should come to

me?" (Lk. 1:43). The following chart summarizes this strong correlation between 2 Samuel 6 and Luke 1.

2 Samuel 6	Luke 1
David arose and went back to Judah (v. 2)	Mary arose and went to the hill country of Judah (v. 39)
How can the ark of the Lord come to me (v. 9)	And why is this granted me, that the mother of my Lord should come to me? (v. 43)
House of Obed-edom (v. 10)	House of Zechariah (v. 40)
Ark there three months (v. 11)	Mary stays three months with Elizabeth (v. 56)
David rejoices (v. 12)	Mary's spirit rejoices (v. 47)
shouting (v. 15)	loud cry (v. 42)
leaping and dancing (v. 16)	the babe leaps in Elizabeth's womb (v. 41)

Bearing Christ's Presence

The quantitative poverty of biblical narratives specifically concerning Mary is compensated by the qualitative wealth of meaning in those narratives. The few words that Luke gives us about Mary are like gems: rare, but rich in beauty. One facet of this gem shows Mary's mediating role in salvation history. In the Old Testament the Spirit of God, the Shekina, would overshadow and rest on the ark (Ex. 40:34 *et seq.*), thus revealing to the people the presence of God. In Luke's Gospel, the angel Gabriel tells Mary that the Holy Spirit will come upon her and overshadow her (Lk. 1:35). The primary role of the ark in the Old Covenant was to mediate the presence of God to Israel, and the role of Mary is to bear Christ to the world.

This role of bearing Christ to the world is a role that all Christians are to share with Mary. We are all called to imitate Jesus' most faithful discile in bearing the presence of God to the world. Saint Paul reminds us and the Corinthians that our bodies are temples of the Holy Spirit (1 Cor. 6:19). When we receive the Eucharist, we receive into our bodies the true body and blood, soul and divinity of Jesus Christ. We become like Mary, who held the flesh and blood of the Christ child in her body. We should approach the most Blessed Sacrament with the fear and rejoicing with which David brings the first ark of the covenant into Jerusalem. When we receive this most precious gift, Mary's words should be our own, "My soul magnifies the Lord, and my spirit rejoices in God my Savior, for he has regarded the low estate of his handmaiden" (Lk. 1:46-48).

Spiritual Warfare

In the Old Testament, the ark also served as a mighty weapon in Israel's holy wars. Israel's holy warfare was fought in conquering and maintaining the Promised Land. The Book of Numbers tells us that "whenever the ark set out, Moses said, 'Arise, O LORD, and let thy enemies be scattered; and let them that hate thee flee before thee'" (Num. 10:35).

Two significant details about the ark are revealed in this passage. First, as we saw above, the ark is associated with God's presence, demonstrated by the words "before thee." Second, the ark is closely associated with battle. In fact, chapter ten of Numbers describes only two things, the ark and the army of Israel. This relationship between the ark and warfare is found throughout the Old Testament. The battle and fall of Jericho (Josh. 6) exemplify the power of the ark in battle. The Israelites, led by the Levites carrying the ark, circle the city for seven days. On the last day, at the sound of the horns of the Levites and with the triumphant shout of the Israelites, the city of Jericho falls without a single casualty. This incident teaches that the Promised Land is to be conquered more by liturgical and spiritual warfare than by catapults and swords. The power and presence of God, mediated by the ark, provides Israel's victory.

The ark played a significant role in Israel's warfare just as Mary has a decisive role in the Church's spiritual battles. The Promised Land is a figure of heaven; the ark is a figure of Mary who is key to the spiritual combat we must fight in order to gain heaven. In fact, the role of the ark in warfare appears to be alluded to in Saint John's description of Mary in Revelation 12.

At the end of Revelation 11, just before John sees the vision of the woman crowned with twelve stars, the heavens open up and in God's Temple the ark of the covenant is revealed. This scene is continued in Revelation 12, but standing in the place of the ark is the woman crowned with stars. (It is helpful to remember that the Scriptures originally contained no chapter or verse divisions. These were added hundreds of years later. What we see as chapter 12 should be read as originally written, right on the heels of chapter 11.) The woman and the ark of the covenant are revealed as one and the same. Upon this revelation of the new ark of the covenant, the great battle in the heavens begins.

The Church, which is the new Israel, understands that the role of the ark of the covenant has been transferred to Mary. She who bore Christ's presence to the world is the spiritual mother of all Christians (Rev. 12:17). She is granted power over and protection from the dreaded dragon, who cannot prevail against her (Rev. 12:13-16).

Mercy Seat

Another feature of the ark in the Old Testament is that it was seen as the throne of God. As noted, when the ark was carried by the Levites it was carried in a procession, lifted up by long poles. This was the way that royalty was carried in ancient times. Yahweh was the king of Israel, and His throne was believed to be the ark of the covenant. Thus Psalm 68, which commemorates the ark, says that, "Thy solemn processions are seen, O God, the processions of my God, my King, into the sanctuary" (v. 24).

When God gave Moses the instructions for the ark, He commanded that the "mercy seat" be made upon the ark (Ex. 24:17 *et seq.*). Israel was to seek the mercy of God from His throne upon the ark, the seat of mercy (cf. 1 Kings 8:21-53; Ex. 25:22). If the ark of the covenant was the place where Israel sought the mercy of God, it is easy for Christians to see the parallel with Mary. We fly to the "Mother of Mercy" and beg for God's mercy upon us. Just as the ark of old served as the throne of God's presence, so too Mary serves as the throne of God as she holds the Christ child in her lap. This touching scene is often depicted in Christian art. Thus Mary is also known as the "Seat of Wisdom." Both the ark and Mary are intended by Our Heavenly Father to bring us into a deeper encounter with Jesus Christ and His tender mercy.

The Church, which is the new Israel, understands that the role of the ark of the covenant has been transferred to Mary. She continues to reflect Christ's light into history. She also is our weapon against the powers of hell. By the help of the Rosary and other Marian prayers, and through our meditation on Mary's bearing of Christ to the world, we can have confidence that our new ark of the covenant will help bring about the victory of Jesus in our lives.

God's Masterpiece

By the overshadowing of the Holy Spirit, Mary becomes the new and paramount ark. Just as the ark of the covenant was made holy by its precious contents, so Mary is made holy by the Son of God made flesh within her womb and the indwelling of the Holy Spirit. If the ark of the covenant was rightfully revered in Israel's liturgy, it should be no surprise that the ark of the New Covenant, Mary, has a place of great honor in the liturgy and life of the new Israel, the Church. After all, God has placed her in the midst of His heavenly temple and has crowned her with a crown of twelve stars. In John's vision, a third of the angels, along with their leader, the great dragon, are thrown down from the heaven, whereas the woman is raised up on the wings of eagles. Clearly

God has thrown down "the mighty from their thrones, and exalted those of low degree" (Lk. 1:52). Therefore the Catechism declares that: "Mary, the all-holy ever-virgin Mother of God, is the masterwork of the mission of the Son and the Spirit in the fullness of time" (no. 721). As God's "masterwork," it is no wonder why all generations call her blessed.

CHAPTER VI

Treat Her Like a Queen
The Biblical Call to Honor Mary as Royal Mother

EDWARD P. SRI

No one treats Mary like a queen more than Catholics.

We honor her as our royal mother in numerous ways. We sing the famous "Hail Holy Queen enthroned above . . ." When we pray the Rosary, we honor Mary as the crowned queen in the fifth glorious mystery. All over the world, statues and paintings express the Blessed Mother's royal office by portraying her with a crown on her head. We even have a special feast day dedicated specifically to celebrate her queenship over heaven and earth (August 22).

Yet all this royal attention given to the mother of Jesus might sound scandalous to some non-Catholic ears. After all, isn't calling Mary "queen" going a little too far? The Bible doesn't mention anything about there being a *queen* in God's kingdom. Paying homage to Mary as some type of royal mother seems to detract from the absolute kingship of Jesus Christ which belongs to Him alone! And besides, how could Mary be a queen since she is not the *wife* of the king Jesus, but only His mother?

These are good questions, and they deserve good answers. It is true that Christians throughout the centuries have honored

Mary as some type of royal mother. From early Church Fathers such as Saint Jerome, Saint Augustine, and Saint Ephrem to modern teachings from Vatican II, Pope John Paul II, and the *Catechism of the Catholic Church*, Christians throughout the ages have recognized Mary's queenship. But where did this idea come from? Where does Scripture teach that Mary should be honored as queen?

There is one biblical theme which sheds light on these issues and serves as a key for unlocking the mystery of Mary's queenship. This theme is the Old Testament tradition of the "queen mother" in the Davidic kingdom.[1]

There's No One Like Mom

You probably have seen this many times before. You're watching a big football game on national television, and some star player scores a clutch touchdown. His teammates quickly surround him jumping up and down together for a grand celebration of male bonding in the end zone. At the height of the celebration, when the TV zooms in for a close-up, you see him look into the camera and scream out two words: "Hi Mom!"

You've got to wonder: Many of these football players probably have wives or girlfriends at home watching them on TV. Why don't these guys say "hi" to *them*? Why is it that *mom* always seems to receive the special attention?

We find a similar situation in ancient Israel. Even then, mothers were singled out for special treatment by their sons, especially in the royal household of the kingdom of Judah. Among all the ladies in the kingdom, there was no one more honored than the king's mother. Even the king's wife could not compete with the prestigious role of the mother.

---

[1] Cf. N. Andreasen, "The Role of Queen Mother in Israelite Society," *Catholic Biblical Quarterly*, vol. 45 (1983), 180.

What made the mother of the king so special? In the Davidic monarchy, as well as in other ancient kingdoms in the Near East, the king's mother held the most important office in his royal court. She influenced political, economic, and liturgical affairs in the kingdom, and she played a key part in the process of dynastic succession. What is most striking, however, is the fact that she even ruled as queen. It was not the king's *wife* who held the queenship, but his *mother*!

Many Wives, Only One Mother

The great preeminence of the king's mother may seem odd from our modern Western perspective. Today, we generally think of a queen as being the *wife* of a king. However, when we consider the fact that most ancient Near Eastern kings practiced polygamy and had large harems, the idea of a queen mother makes a lot of sense. Think of King Solomon, who had 700 wives (1 Kings 11:3). Imagine the chaos in the royal court if all 700 wives were awarded the queenship! But since each king had only one *mother*, one can see the practical wisdom in bestowing the queenship upon her.

This background is crucial for understanding what the Bible teaches about Mary's queenship. If we search the Scriptures for a royal woman like the queens in modern Western monarchies, we won't find her. Yet, once we grasp the biblical concept of the queen mother, Mary's royal office will jump off the pages of the New Testament and call us to a profound relationship with our queenly mother in the kingdom of Jesus.

The Queen Mother

In the Davidic kingdom, when a new king assumed the throne, his mother was given the special title *gebirah*, which in Hebrew means "great lady" or "queen." As queen mother, she possessed the second most powerful position in the kingdom— second only to the king himself.

Since the queen mother was both the wife of the previous monarch and the mother of the current king, she stood as a

symbol of the king's royalty, tying him to his father's royal
blood. In this sense, she guaranteed the legitimacy of the king's
place in the dynastic line of succession.

> On the throne, the queen mother represented the king's conti-
> nuity with the past, the visible affirmation of God's ongoing
> plan for His people, the channel through which the Lord's
> dynastic promise to David was fulfilled.[2]

A number of Old Testament passages reflect the important role
of the queen mother in the Davidic kingdom. For example, take
the Books of 1 & 2 Kings. These books tell about the various monarchs who ruled over the Israelites. Strikingly, almost every time
the narrative introduces a new king in Judah it mentions the king's
mother as well, highlighting her part in the dynastic succession.

At the end of 2 Kings, when Babylon conquered the kingdom
of Judah, the narrator describes how King Jehoiachin surrendered
the members of the royal court to the king of Babylon. The
narrator puts the queen mother at the head of his list of those
surrendered: "Jehoiachin the king of Judah gave himself up to
the king of Babylon, himself, *and his mother*, and his servants,
and his princes, and his palace officials" (2 Kings 24:12). What is
significant is that the queen mother was considered so important
to the kingdom that she was the first official in the royal court
listed among those surrendered to the Babylonians.

A Woman with Authority

In ancient Israel, the queen mother was no mere figurehead.
Rather, she held an actual office with real authority in the kingdom. In fact, the prophet Jeremiah described how she shared in
the king's rule over the people and even possessed a throne and
a crown of her own—symbolic of her royal power.

---

[2] George T. Montague, S.M., *Our Father, Our Mother* (Steubenville, OH: Franciscan
University Press, 1990), 92.

> Say to the king and the queen mother: "Take a lowly seat,
> for your beautiful *crown* has come down from your head. . . .
> Lift up your eyes and see those who come from the north.
> Where is the flock that was given you, your beautiful flock?"
> (Jer. 13:18, 20).

In this passage, Jeremiah forecasts the imminent fall of the kingdom of Judah. But in doing so, he reveals the great authority of the queen mother. The prophecy describes how the "flock" of Israelites will by taken away from the current Jewish monarchs and will be handed over to the invading Babylonians.

What is important to note is that this prophecy is addressed to both the king *and the queen mother*. Thus, when God says "your beautiful flock" will be taken away, He is referring to the fact that the king and his royal mother shepherded the people *together*. But because of their unfaithfulness, *both* will lose their flocks. Both will lose their thrones ("take a lowly seat") and their crowns will be taken away. This passage clearly reveals how the queen mother had a unique share in her son's rule over the flock of Israelites. She had a position important enough for God to single out in this prophecy of judgment.

At the King's Right Hand

Probably the best example of the queen mother's importance would be that of Bathsheba, the wife of David and mother of Solomon. A number of scholars have noted the preeminence of Bathsheba's position in the kingdom once she became queen mother during Solomon's rule.

Compare, on one hand, the humble attitude of Bathsheba as spouse of King David, and on the other hand, her majestic dignity when she becomes mother of the next king, Solomon. When she was simply spouse of King David, Bathsheba approached the king like most subjects in the kingdom would: She bowed with her face to the ground and honored her husband David when she entered his royal chamber (cf. 1 Kings 1:16-17, 31).

But something far different happened when her son Solomon

assumed the throne and she became the queen mother. Notice the glorious reception she received when meeting with her royal son.

> So Bathsheba went to King Solomon, to speak to him on behalf of Adonijah. And the king rose to meet her, and bowed down to her; then he sat on his throne, and had a seat brought for the king's mother; and she sat on his right. Then she said, "I have one small request to make of you; do not refuse me." And the king said to her, "Make your request, my mother; for I will not refuse you" (1 Kings 2:19-20).

This account reveals the sovereign prerogatives of the queen mother. Before, when she was just the spouse of the king, *she* had to bow down before David. However, now as queen mother, it is *the king* who rose and bowed to greet *her*!

But that's not all. After this royal greeting, King Solomon did something even more remarkable. He gave his mother Bathsheba a seat at his right hand. This was not a simple courtesy of offering his mother a chair. This action was charged with royal symbolism. In the Bible, the right hand is the ultimate place of honor. For example, Psalm 110 describes how the messiah will sit at God's right hand and rule over all nations. Similarly, the Book of Hebrews portrays Christ as sitting at the right hand of the Father, ruling over all creation, exalted above all angels and saints (Heb. 1:13; cf. Catechism, nos. 663-64).

As such, Solomon does not offer the queen mother any ordinary seat. Rather, he gives her the most powerful position he could offer in the entire kingdom. Sitting at the king's right hand, the queen mother clearly has a unique share in the king's royal authority.

A Mother's Touch: Advocate

This account of Bathsheba's majestic meeting with Solomon also demonstrates one key way the queen mother exerted influence in the kingdom: as an advocate for the people. As a powerful intercessor, the queen mother had the special job of bringing the petitions of the people to her royal son.

In 1 Kings 2:17, we find a man named Adonijah who recognized the queen mother's important position as advocate. Notice how he confidently asked Bathsheba (the reigning queen mother) to take a special petition for him to King Solomon. He said to her: "Pray ask King Solomon—*he will not refuse you*—to give me Abishag the Shunammite as my wife" (1 Kings 2:17). Adonijah knew the king always listened to the queen mother. She was a powerful advocate, and that is why he confidently asked her to intercede on his behalf.

Solomon's response to Bathsheba further demonstrates the queen mother's powerful influence. When Bathsheba brought this petition to Solomon, the king replied, "Make your request, my mother; for *I will not refuse you*" (1 Kings 2:20). Solomon's words reveal the king's solemn commitment to the queen mother's petitions.[3] All this, of course, foreshadows how Mary as queen mother serves as our advocate, constantly interceding on our behalf before the throne of her Son, King Jesus.

Queen Mother in Prophecy

Given the preeminent role of the queen mother in the Davidic kingdom, it is not surprising that she would appear in some Old Testament prophecies about the coming of the messiah and his renewed kingdom. One example is Isaiah 7:14.

---

[3] "The fact that Solomon denies the request in no way discredits the influence of the *gebirah*. Adonijah wanted Abishag the Shunammite for the treacherous purpose of taking over the kingdom from Solomon. [Taking the king's concubine was a sign of usurping the throne in the ancient Near East. For example, see how Absalom, in his attempt to take the throne from David, took his concubines (2 Sam. 16:20-23).] Thus *the wickedness of Adonijah's intention is the reason for denial, which in no way reflects negatively upon the gebirah's power to intercede. The narrative bears out the fact that the king normally accepted the gebirah's request*, thus Solomon says, 'Ask, I will not refuse you.' To say then that this illustrates the weakness of the *gebirah's* ability to intercede would be to miss the whole point of the narrative, which tells how Adonijah uses the queen mother's position in an attempt to become king." Timothy Gray, "God's Word and Mary's Royal Office," *Miles Immaculatae* 13 (1995), no. 16, 381, emphasis added. For more on the political symbolism of taking a member of the king's harem, see Roland de Vaux, *Ancient Israel* (New York: McGraw-Hill, 1961), 116.

Isaiah uttered this prophecy in a time when the Davidic kingdom was in big trouble. Two foreign powers were threatening Jerusalem and plotting to overthrow King Ahaz, who feared that his days were numbered and that the great Davidic dynasty might come to an end with him.

However, in this famous prophecy of Isaiah, God offered Ahaz a sign that the kingdom would endure through this trial and the dynasty would continue through one of his sons:

> Hear then, O house of David! . . . the Lord himself will give you a sign. Behold, a virgin shall conceive and bear a son, and shall call his name Immanu-el (Is. 7:13-14).[4]

On one level, this passage points to a son of King Ahaz (Hezekiah), who will assume the throne and turn away the foreign armies. The biblical title Immanu-el, often rendered "Emmanuel," means "God with us," and fittingly so. For God truly will be with this son as a pledge that the Davidic dynasty will continue despite the threats of invading nations.

At the same time, Isaiah tells how the royal son in this prophecy also refers to an even greater king who will come in the distant future—a king who will sit "upon the throne of David, and over his kingdom, to establish it, and to uphold it with justice and with righteousness from this time forth and for evermore" (Is. 9:7; cf. 11:1-16). This points to no one else but Jesus, the Messiah.

For our purposes, we should note how the mother plays an important part in this prophecy: "a virgin shall conceive and bear a son." Who is this virgin mother? Why is she important?

Since the oracle is addressed specifically to the Davidic household and concerns the continuation of the dynasty, the young woman who bears a royal son clearly would be a queen

---

[4] Alternative translation provided in footnote i of the RSVCE.

mother. In this light, we see that Isaiah not only foretold the coming of the Messiah, but he also described the important role of the virgin queen mother who would bear Him forth into the world. Thus, the Scriptures point ahead and build expectation for the coming of this great mother and her royal Son. The stage is set for Mary and Jesus.

The Woman of the House

Luke's Gospel has much to say about Mary's royal office. In fact, in the scene of the Annunciation, Luke shows us that Mary was given the vocation to be the queen mother in the kingdom of Jesus.

When the angel Gabriel appeared to Mary, she was told she would become the mother of a royal Son who would restore the Davidic kingdom. This child would be the fulfillment of many prophecies which foretold how the Messiah would establish God's kingdom and reign forever (2 Sam. 7; Ps. 2, 72, 89). First, the angel Gabriel is said to appear to a virgin betrothed to a man *"of the house of David"* (Lk. 1:27). Then, the angel told Mary:

> And behold, you will conceive in your womb and bear a son, and you shall call his name Jesus. He will be great, and will be called Son of the Most High; and the Lord God will give to him the throne of his father David, and he will reign over the house of Jacob for ever; and of his kingdom there will be no end (Lk. 1:31-33).

If an ancient Jew heard of a woman in the house of David giving birth to a new Davidic king, he would easily conclude that she was a queen mother. And that's exactly the vocation to which Mary is being called at the Annunciation. She is the queen mother of the one who will sit on "the throne of his father David" and of whose "kingdom there will be no end."

This royal office of Mary's is made even more explicit in the next scene of Luke's Gospel, when Mary visits her cousin Elizabeth who also is with child.

"The Mother of My Lord"

Did you know that the "Hail Mary" is a biblical prayer which honors Our Lady specifically as queen mother? In the middle of this famous Catholic prayer, we say, "Holy Mary, Mother of God, pray for us sinners . . ." The phrase "Mother of God" is derived from the scene of the Visitation when Elizabeth greets Mary saying, "[W]hy is this granted me, that the *mother of my Lord* should come to me?" (Lk. 1:43).

This title which Elizabeth bestows upon Mary is packed with great queenly significance. In the royal court language of the ancient Near East, the title "mother of my Lord" was used to address the queen mother of the reigning king. The king himself was addressed as "my Lord" (cf. 2 Sam. 24:21), and the queen mother would have been called "mother of my Lord." In using this title, Elizabeth recognizes the great dignity of Mary's role as queen mother.

These are the words which Catholics echo when they pray the "Hail Mary." Thus, when Catholics honor Mary as queen, we are simply following the example of Elizabeth, who was the first person in the Bible explicitly to recognize Mary's queenly office as the "mother of my Lord."

Four Kings and a Mother

Like Luke, Matthew also draws attention to Mary's queenship, but he does so in a subtle way. In a famous scene from chapter 2 of his Gospel, Matthew singles out Mary as being with the child when the three magi come to adore the newborn King. Notice how Joseph is conspicuously not even mentioned in this scene: ". . . going into the house they [the three magi] saw the child with Mary his mother, and they fell down and worshiped him" (Mt. 2:11).

Why does Matthew zoom in on Jesus and Mary and leave Joseph out of the picture at this point? All throughout the narrative in Matthew 1-2, Joseph is much more prominent than Mary. Matthew traces Jesus' genealogy through Joseph. The angel appears to Joseph three times. It is Joseph who leads the Holy Family to Bethlehem, to Egypt, and back to Israel. From this we can see Joseph often takes the spotlight in the first few scenes of Matthew's Gospel.

However, in this particular episode when the magi come to honor Jesus, Mary takes center stage and Joseph fades into the background. Why? Because it shows the importance of Mary as queen mother. As Scripture scholar Raymond Brown explains:

> [S]ince the magi story puts so much emphasis on homage paid to a Davidic king in Bethlehem of Judah, "the child with his mother" might evoke the peculiar importance given to the queen-mother . . . of a newborn or newly installed king in the Davidic dynasty.[5]

It is quite significant that just when Jesus' kingship is being recognized for the first time by these three magi, Matthew highlights the close relationship between the infant King and His queen mother. At the very beginning of Jesus' life, Matthew draws attention to the queen mother's being right by the king's side, sharing in His kingship—just like the queen mothers of old in the kingdom of David.[6]

The Woman of the Apocalypse

Finally, we turn to the Apostle John's dramatic vision of "a woman clothed with the sun" in the Book of Revelation.

> And a great portent appeared in heaven, a woman clothed with the sun, with the moon under her feet, and on her head a crown of twelve stars; she was with child and she cried out in her pangs of birth, in anguish for delivery (Rev. 12:1-2).

---

[5] Raymond Brown, *The Birth of the Messiah* (New York: Doubleday, 1993), 192.
[6] A. Serra, "Regina: Ulteriore Elaborazione Biblica sulla Regalità di Maria," in *Nuvo Dizionario di Mariologia*, ed. S. De Fiores (Milan: Edizioni Pauline, 1996), 1073.

Who is this majestic woman crowned with twelve stars? In order to discover who this mysterious lady is, we must first recognize the identity of her Son.

In one short sentence a few verses later, John tells us who this child is, but he does so in a way that some modern readers might not catch at first glance. All John says is that the child was taken up to heaven, seated on a throne, and destined to "rule all the nations with a rod of iron" (Rev. 12:5). Yet, without even saying the child's name, this brief description shouts out His identity. As discussed in the preceding chapters, John is unmistakably alluding to Psalm 2:8-9—one of the most famous psalms telling how God will exalt the coming Messiah-King: "Ask of me, and I will make *the nations* your heritage, and the ends of the earth your possession. You shall break them *with a rod of iron.*"

By applying this messianic imagery to the child in Revelation 12, John shows us that the woman's son is the long-awaited Messiah-King. If that is the case, then who is the royal woman giving birth to this child? Who is the mother of the Messiah? Clearly, it is Mary.[7] Here, we see Mary in her role as queen mother in all her magnificence alongside her royal Son Jesus reigning in heaven.

---

[7] Although the identification of Mary as the "woman" of Revelation may seem self-evident, some have interpreted the woman as merely a symbol either for the Old Testament People of Israel or for the New Testament Church. They conclude that the woman is not an individual (i.e., Mary), but only a symbol for God's people.

However, this "either-or" proposition is foreign to the biblical worldview in which individuals often symbolically represent collective groups (e.g., Adam represented all humanity—Rom. 5:19; Jacob stood for all of Israel—Ps. 44:4). Given this biblical notion called "corporate personality," the woman in Revelation 12 should be understood as *both* an individual (Mary) *and* a symbol for the People of God. Finally, since the other two main characters in this vision are generally recognized primarily as individuals (the child = Jesus; the dragon = the devil), it seems quite unlikely that the third main character, the woman, is not an individual, but only a symbol for a corporate group. Rather, recognizing the woman as Mary makes the most sense out of the text and at the same time is open to viewing her secondarily as a symbol for Israel or the Church.

A Crown of Twelve Stars

With this background, we find in Revelation 12 the most splendid picture of Mary's royal office. She is portrayed as queen mother reigning with her triumphant Son in heaven. Like the queen mothers of old, she wears a crown on her head, symbolizing her royal authority. Yet, the number of stars in her crown tells us that her queenship far surpasses the majesty and authority of the queen mothers back in the kingdom of Judah. The twelve stars recall not only the twelve tribes of Israel, but also the twelve apostles, who serve as the foundation of Christ's everlasting kingdom, the Church. Thus, wearing a crown of twelve stars, Mary is seen as having authority not simply over the kingdom of Judah, but over the kingdom of Christ—a kingdom which goes far beyond time and space. Indeed, Mary is queen of heaven and earth!

Also, the imagery of the sun, moon, and stars surrounding Mary bring to mind Joseph's famous dream in the Old Testament. In this dream, the patriarch Joseph envisioned the sun, moon, and eleven stars bowing down before him—a foreshadowing of the royal authority he would have over his father, mother, and eleven brothers when he would rise to become second in command over Pharaoh's kingdom in Egypt (Gen. 37:9). Thus, the vision of Mary clothed with the sun, sitting above the moon, and crowned with stars over her head would recall the royal imagery of Joseph's dream and point to her own preeminent position in God's kingdom.

Mary: Our Queen Mother

We have seen how the Old Testament queen mother tradition serves as an important background for understanding Mary's royal office. Indeed, the New Testament portrays Mary as the queen mother *par excellence*. Just as the queen mother in the Davidic dynasty held the highest position of honor and influence, second only to the king, so too does Mary as the new queen mother hold a preeminent position in the new kingdom, second only to Christ. Therefore, Catholic prayers, hymns, and art recognizing Mary's queenship should be seen as fitting responses to the biblical call for all Christians to honor Mary in her royal office.[8]

We must emphasize, however, that in honoring Mary as queen mother, we do not take anything away from Christ. In fact, understanding Mary as queen mother emphasizes how *she is completely subordinate to Christ*. Just as the queen mother's royal office was based entirely on her son's kingship, so too Mary's exalted position in the kingdom depends entirely on her Son, Jesus. In this light, Mary's queenship in no way diminishes Christ's kingship, but rests completely on it. In fact, *we exalt Jesus even more by honoring her as queen* because in doing so, we praise Him for the great work He has done in her and through her queenship. As Vatican II taught, "Mary's function as mother of men in no way obscures or diminishes this unique mediation of Christ, but rather shows its power" (LG 60; cf. Catechism, no. 970).

Finally, understanding Mary as queen mother sheds light on her important intercessory role in the Christian life.[9] Just like the queen mother of the Davidic kingdom, Mary continues to serve as an advocate for the people in the kingdom of God today. This is why we can ask Mary to pray for us. As queen mother, she is

---

[8] In what sense does Mary participate in Christ's kingship? Recall that Jesus promised to share His reign with *all* the disciples who follow Him in humble service and perseverance to the end (Mt. 19:28-30; Lk. 22:26-30; 2 Tim. 2:11-12; Rev. 3:20-21). As a model disciple of Christ, Mary simply has a unique, preeminent share in her Son's rule in the kingdom. She offered her life as a humble servant of the Lord (Lk. 1:38, 48; cf. Jn. 2:3-5; 19:25-27), and thus she is exalted (Lk. 1:46-55; cf. Rev. 12:1). Therefore, Mary's queenship is not something far removed from the Christian life. It is not simply an exalted position in heaven which we are only to marvel at from a distance. Rather, Mary's queenship stands as an icon, an eschatological sign, of what all Christians are called to: to share in Christ's glorious victory over sin and death (LG 68; Catechism, no. 972).

[9] For example, we can see Mary serving as an advocate at the wedding feast of Cana (Jn. 2:1-11). There she intercedes for the needs of the wedding party. Like a queen mother, Mary petitions her kingly Son for help, and Jesus responds by changing the water into wine.

the most powerful intercessor in Christ's kingdom and is able to take our needs to the throne of her Son. Therefore, let us approach our queen mother with confidence, knowing that she faithfully carries our petitions to her royal Son Jesus, who responds to her as Solomon did to Bathsheba, saying: "I will not refuse you" (1 Kings 2:20).

Edward P. Sri, S.T.L., is assistant professor of religious studies at Benedictine College in Atchison, Kansas, where he teaches Scripture and theology. He holds a licentiate from the Angelicum in Rome, where he is currently a doctoral candidate. He is also a regional coordinator for the Fellowship Of Catholic University Students (FOCUS) and the author of Mystery of the Kingdom *(Emmaus Road Publishing), a study of St. Matthew's Gospel. He resides in Atchison, Kansas, with his wife Elizabeth.*

CHAPTER VII

Always a Virgin

LEON J. SUPRENANT, JR.

The Catholic Church has always taught that Mary was a virgin before, during, and after the birth of Christ. Mary conceived Jesus in her womb by the power of the Holy Spirit without the loss of her virginity. She remained a virgin in giving birth to Jesus, such that the miraculous birth did not diminish her virginal integrity but sanctified it (cf. LG 57). Following the birth of Jesus, Mary remained a virgin for the rest of her earthly life, until such time as she was taken body and soul into heaven, where she reigns as queen (*ibid.*, 59).

Mary's virginity includes a constant virginal disposition and freedom from disordered sexual desires as well as physical integrity. The Church's teaching refers primarily, but not exclusively, to her bodily integrity. Even so, Mary's physical virginity must be seen as a symbol and manifestation of an interior, spiritual virginity, inasmuch as the body expresses the person (cf. Catechism, no. 364).

Mary's virginity is no mere historical accident; it permeates every aspect of her life. In other words, this Marian dogma is not simply an abstract formula to be memorized, but rather tells us

who our Blessed Mother is. Just as Mary was not only immac-
ulately conceived, but is, as was further confirmed at Lourdes,
the Immaculate Conception, so also Mary's virginity is not a
mere attribute or description, but part of her very being.[1]

Returning to the Source

In examining Mary's Perpetual Virginity, or any Church
teaching, the most fundamental question is "How do we know
this is true?" We do not gain such knowledge through intuition
or merely human effort or reasoning, but through the "obedience
of faith" that we give to God who has revealed the truth to us
(Rom. 1:5; 16:26; cf. DV 5).

In identifying this revealed truth, we must acknowledge that
Scripture and Tradition make up a single sacred deposit of the
Word of God, which is entrusted to the Church (DV 10). We
must further recognize that the task of safeguarding (cf. 1 Tim.
6:20) and authentically interpreting the Word of God, oral or
written, has been entrusted to the Magisterium ("teaching
office") of the Church alone (DV 10).

The dogma of Mary's Perpetual Virginity brings to light
two distinct errors that are rooted in misconceptions concerning the nature of divine Revelation. The first error is a *sola
scriptura* ("Scripture alone") approach that collapses the Word
of God to merely that which has been written, thereby denying
the legitimate role of Tradition and the Magisterium. Curiously,
such a position, developed during the Protestant Reformation, is
not taught in Scripture. Indeed, the testimony of Scripture
appears otherwise. For example, in 2 Thessalonians 2:15, Saint
Paul exhorts his followers to "stand firm and hold to the traditions which you were taught by us, either by word of mouth or

---

[1] This point is exemplified by Marian prayers (e.g., "O most gracious Virgin Mary," "O
sweet Virgin Mary," etc.), the celebration of Mary as *Aeiparthenos* (the "Ever-virgin") in
the liturgy (Catechism, no. 499; LG 52), and even papal references (e.g., Pope John Paul
II, Encyclical Letter Mother of the Redeemer *Redemptoris Mater*, no. 41, quoting Pius
XII, calls Mary "the Immaculate Virgin").

by letter." In 1 Timothy 3:15, Saint Paul further states that the *Church* is "the pillar and bulwark of the truth."

Sola scriptura rightly emphasizes that Scripture is God's Word to us. However, this approach attempts to understand Scripture apart from Mother Church, even though the Church was "alive" for decades before the New Testament in its entirety was written, and for centuries before the Church definitively determined which texts were inspired.

The other error is an approach that fails to accord the necessary weight and dignity to Scripture. This error can manifest itself in many forms, often so as to render "truth" an elusive, if not illusory, reality.[2] An example would be an inclination to relegate the infancy narratives to the level of pious fables that are merely the product of the second or third generation Church.

Against such an "enlightened" modern interpretation of Scripture, Vatican II, citing earlier magisterial documents, affirms "that the books of Scripture, firmly, faithfully, and without error, teach that truth which God, for the sake of our salvation, wished to see confided to the Sacred Scriptures" (DV 11; Catechism, no. 107). The sacred authors consigned to writing what the Holy Spirit wanted, and no more, and did so without error (DV 11; Catechism, no. 106). Pope Leo XIII, in a document cited twice in *Dei Verbum*, no. 11, unequivocally confirmed that this is the "ancient and unchanging faith of the Church."[3] As if this reaffirmation of biblical inerrancy were not enough, Vatican II then "unhesitatingly affirms" the historicity of the Gospels (DV 19).

Aside from the relative merits of particular methods of Scripture study, the simple fact remains that the charism of authentic interpretation resides with the Magisterium and not the supposed "experts." While theologians can provide a tremendous service in helping us understand what we believe, any scholarship

---

[2] Cf. Pope St. Pius X, Encyclical Letter On the Doctrines of the Modernists *Pascendi Dominici Gregis* (1907), nos. 3, 24-26.

[3] Pope Leo XIII, Encyclical Letter On the Study of Holy Scripture *Providentissimus Deus* (1893), no. 20.

that calls into question established doctrine, or even produces conclusions in conflict with doctrines affirmed by the teaching Church, must necessarily be rejected.[4]

In prayerfully studying the Church's teaching on Mary's Perpetual Virginity, we see in action "the supremely wise arrangement of God" (DV 10), whereby Scripture, Tradition, and the Magisterium work together under the action of the Holy Spirit to communicate the truth about Mary to successive generations of Christians.

Mary's Virginity Before the Birth of Christ

Both Matthew 1:18-25 and Luke 1:26-28 provide explicit scriptural evidence for Mary's virginal conception of Jesus.

Saint Matthew describes the virginal conception as a fulfillment of the prophecy of Isaiah 7:14: "Behold, a virgin shall conceive and bear a son, and shall call his name Emmanuel" (Mt. 1:23). Saint Matthew's Gospel is also unique in its presentation of the virginal conception from the perspective of Saint Joseph, to whom an angel appeared to confirm, by a special revelation, the miraculous origin of the child. Many scholars draw the reasonable conclusion that Mary and Joseph were probably aware of the accomplishment of Isaiah's prophecy.[5]

It is clear from Saint Luke's account of the Annunciation that the angel appeared "to a virgin betrothed to a man whose name was Joseph," and that "the virgin's name was Mary" (Lk. 1:27). The critical verses, however, are verses 34-35, in which Mary asked how this conception would occur—since she was a virgin—and was advised by the angel that she would conceive by the power of the Holy Spirit. If Mary intended to consummate her

---

[4] See generally, Congregation for the Doctrine of the Faith, *Instruction on the Ecclesial Vocation of the Theologian* (Boston: St. Paul Books & Media, 1990).

[5] For example, see Michael J. Gruenthaner, S.J., "Mary in the New Testament," as reproduced in Juniper B. Carol, O.F.M., ed., *Mariology* (Milwaukee: The Bruce Publishing Co., 1955), vol. 1, 91.

relationship with Saint Joseph at some future time, her question would have been nonsensical.[6] The literal-historical sense of these passages, which provide that Mary conceived Jesus without the loss of her virginity, is simply beyond reasonable dispute.

The teaching of the Fathers, dating back to Saint Ignatius of Antioch at the turn of the second century, unanimously supports the teaching of the virginal conception, as does the testimony of the earliest creeds and Marian prayers. The popes seem to take the virginal conception as a given when addressing Mary's virginity during and after Jesus' birth.

Mary's Perpetual Virginity, including the virginal conception of Christ, was affirmed at the Lateran Council under Pope St. Martin I, in which the following canon was promulgated:

> If anyone does not in accord with the Holy Fathers acknowledge that the holy and ever-virgin and immaculate Mary was really and truly the Mother of God, inasmuch as she, in the fullness of time, and without seed, conceived by the Holy Spirit God the Word Himself, who before all time was born of God the Father, and without loss of integrity brought him forth, and after His birth preserved her virginity inviolate, let him be condemned.[7]

It should be noted that the Lateran Council that produced the foregoing canon in 649 was not a general (i.e., ecumenical) council.[8] However, in 681, the sixth ecumenical council (Constantinople III) accepted this canon without question, thereby

---

[6] Fr. Philip J. Donnelly, S.J., defends the Catholic tradition that Mary had consecrated her virginity to God perpetually before the Annunciation, based both on sound exegesis of the text and on the Church's understanding of the text through history, in his article "The Perpetual Virginity of the Mother of God," as reproduced in Carol, *supra*, vol. 2, 234 *et seq.*

[7] Taken from Eamon R. Carroll, O.Carm., "Mary in the Documents of the Magisterium," as reproduced in Carol, *supra*, vol. 1, 13.

[8] The council of 649 was convened by papal authority, but the First Lateran (ecumenical) Council was not convoked until 1123. *Ibid.* See generally, *New Catholic Encyclopedia* (New York: McGraw-Hill Book Co., 1967), vol. 8, 406.

clearly affirming its dogmatic character. Even prior to this definition, the fifth ecumenical council (Constantinople II) in 553 had given Mary the title "ever-virgin."

The teaching was later reaffirmed by other ecumenical councils (Lateran IV, 1214, and Lyons II, 1274). Pope Paul IV in 1555 condemned the following errors:

> that [the Lord] was not conceived of the Holy Spirit according to the flesh in the womb of the most Blessed and ever-virgin Mary, but that his conception in no way differed from the conception of other men, and that he was conceived of the seed of Joseph.[9]

Mary's virginity, and specifically in this context her virginal conception of Christ, continues to be unswervingly proclaimed up to the present time, as one would expect of a dogmatic truth (see generally, Catechism, nos. 496-507).

Objections to the Virginal Conception of Christ

As one commentator emphasizes, since Luke 1:34-35 "[establishes] beyond all doubt the virginal conception of Christ, critics have had no other means of escape in their arbitrary denial of the doctrine than to deny the genuineness and authenticity of these verses."[10] Yet not a single manuscript containing the first chapter of Luke omits verses 34-35. It is rather clear in such a denial that the text is being interpreted according to uncritical, preconceived biases (e.g., the impossibility of miracles and angelic messages, etc.) that are radically divorced from an obedience of faith to divine Revelation.

Some contend that "maiden" or "young woman" would be a better translation of the original Hebrew text of Isaiah 7:14

---

[9] Pope Paul IV, *Cum Quorundum* (1555), as reproduced in John F. Clarkson, S.J., *et al.*, eds., *The Church Teaches* (Rockford, IL: Tan Books and Publishers, Inc., 1973), 206.

[10] Donnelly, "The Perpetual Virginity of the Mother of God," 234.

than "virgin." Leaving aside the relative merits of etymological arguments,[11] the point remains that from the beginning—as reflected in Matthew 1:23—the Church has interpreted Isaiah 7:14 as a prophecy of the virginal conception of Christ in the womb of Mary. The argument made by Saint Justin Martyr in the second century is still instructive today: "If a virginal conception were not the clear, literal sense of the passage, there simply would be no question of a 'sign.'"[12]

The act of calling into question the certainty of biblical truths that have been dogmatically defined by the Church betrays a convergence of several Modernist attitudes identified by the Church last century.[13] Such attitudes unfortunately have resulted in a questioning of the virginal conception in contemporary Catholic circles.[14] This modern doubt, which obviously does not affect the status of the teaching, stems from an attempt to conduct biblical study without considering—and at times systematically rejecting—the inspired, ecclesial nature of Scripture.

---

[11] The Hebrew noun "*alma*" was rendered "*parthenos*" ("virgin") in the Greek Septuagint. It appears that an "alma" in biblical language means an untouched marriageable maiden, so that "parthenos" or "virgin" is a legitimate translation. See Ludwig Ott, *Fundamentals of Catholic Dogma* (Rockford, IL: Tan Books and Publishers, 1974), 204. I suspect the distinction our contemporary Western culture draws between an unmarried young woman and a virgin was not a concern on the part of Isaiah.

[12] As quoted in Reginald Garrigou-Lagrange, O.P., *The Mother of the Savior and Our Interior Life* (St. Louis: B. Herder Book, Co., 1949), 122.

[13] These would include at least a practical denial of Scripture's inerrancy, and the view that Scripture scholars "may reject as false facts the Church holds as most certain." Pope St. Pius X, Syllabus Condemning the Errors of the Modernists *Lamentabili Sane* (1907), no. 23; see also nos. 2, 3, 4, 9, 11, 12, 15, 17, 22, and 24; see generally *Pascendi Dominici Gregis*, no. 3.

[14] For example, there are statements such as that found in the Dutch Catechism that it is only "highly improbable" that Joseph and Mary had other children. Similarly, Fr. Raymond E. Brown, in *The Birth of the Messiah* (Garden City, NY: Image Books, 1977), wrote: "In my book on the virginal conception, . . . I came to the conclusion that the scientifically controllable biblical evidence leaves the question of the historicity of the virginal conception unresolved. The resurvey of the evidence . . . leaves me more convinced of that" (527). Fr. Brown also wrote that "[w]hether or not the infancy narratives were historical . . . Matthew and Luke thought they were appropriate introductions . . . [in which] the evangelists exercised greater freedom of composition" (*ibid.*, 38).

It is beyond dispute that there is no explicit reference to the virginal conception in the New Testament outside the infancy narratives (i.e., Matthew 1-2, Luke 1-2). Scripture scholar Fr. Raymond E. Brown wrote that "it is perfectly proper to speak of the silence of the rest of the New Testament about the virginal conception because not a single one of the 'implicit references' has any compelling force."[15]

This alleged "silence" is important because of the Modernist charge that the virginal conception was unknown to—or not yet "invented" by—the first generation of Christians. After all, the supposedly earliest New Testament writings (Saint Mark's Gospel and Saint Paul's letters) make no mention of a virginal conception.

This line of discussion again betrays a misunderstanding of the sources of Revelation. In any event, the point remains that the Church's teaching on the virginal conception is, at minimum, not in conflict with Saint Mark and Saint Paul. This issue is beautifully laid to rest in the Catechism:

> People are sometimes troubled by the silence of St. Mark's Gospel and the New Testament Epistles about Jesus' virginal conception. Some might wonder if we were merely dealing with legends or theological constructs not claiming to be history. To this we must respond: Faith in the virginal conception of Jesus met with the lively opposition, mockery, or incomprehension of non-believers, Jews and pagans alike; so it could hardly have been motivated by pagan mythology or by some adaptation to the ideas of the age. The meaning of this event is accessible only to faith, which understands in it the "connection of these mysteries with one another[.]" . . . St. Ignatius of Antioch already bears witness to this connection: "Mary's virginity and giving birth, and even the Lord's death escaped the notice of the prince of this world: these three mysteries worthy of proclamation were accomplished in God's silence" (no. 498, footnotes omitted).

---

[15] Brown, *The Birth of the Messiah*, 521.

The Virgin Birth

The Church has traditionally understood Mary's virginity during birth as meaning that Jesus passed from His mother's womb into the light of day without the womb's being opened. In other words, Mary gave birth without the destruction of the physical signs of virginity possessed by one who is virgin in conception, and without labor pains and other infirmities (e.g., rupturing, bleeding, etc.) involved in childbearing after the fall.[16] It was, in reality, a "miraculous birth,"[17] which relates more to her role in the new creation—and thus her Immaculate Conception and Assumption—rather than her virginity before and after.

The teaching that Mary gave birth without the loss of her physical virginity has been clearly taught throughout the life of the Church. While this teaching "protects" the miraculous nature of Christ's birth, in turn the miraculous birth points to a physical integrity that goes beyond the mere absence of sexual relations, which further is a sign of Mary's interior virginity. Yet Mary's virginity during birth is fundamentally—albeit not exclusively— a biological statement, and thus a stumbling block to those who would systematically exclude the possibility of miracles.[18]

There are several Old Testament images that point to Mary's virginity during birth. For example, Saint Ambrose refers to Mary

---

[16] Very Rev. Gerard Owens, C.Ss.R., "Our Lady's Virginity in the Birth of Jesus," *Marian Studies* (1956), vol. 7, 44. *Catechism of the Council of Trent* (South Bend, IN: Marian Publications, 1972) further provides: "[P]reserving her virginal integrity inviolate [Mary] brought forth Jesus the Son of God without experiencing . . . any sense of pain" (46).

[17] Pope Pius XII, Encyclical Letter On the Mystical Body of Christ *Mystici Corporis* (1943), no. 110.

[18] See William B. Smith, "The Theology of the Virginity *in Partu* [during birth] and Its Consequences for the Church's Teaching on Chastity," *Marian Studies* (1971), vol. 22, 76. Msgr. Smith writes that "[i]t is theology's task not to deny or interpret away [the] biological statement [of Mary's virginity during birth,] but to attempt to grasp what it means for God and, therefore, for ourselves" (101-02).

as the closed gate of Ezekiel 44:2.[19] Isaiah refers to the delivery
of a male child born without labor pains (Is. 66:7). Blessed
Thomas of Villanova and others have seen a prefiguring of Mary
in the bush which Moses saw burn without being consumed.[20]

Saint Ambrose wrote on the eve of the Synod of Milan in 390
that the prophecy of Isaiah 7:14 "declares not only that a virgin
shall conceive, but also that a virgin shall bring forth."[21]
Accordingly, Saint Matthew's use of this prophecy in his infancy
narrative (Mt. 1:22-23) at least implies a virgin birth.

It should be noted that Saint Ambrose's interpretation of
Isaiah 7:14 and Matthew 1:22-23 as referring to the virginal
conception *and* the virginal birth represents the interpretation of
the early Church Fathers, and indeed Saint Ambrose's teaching
on Mary's virginity during birth was adopted by the Synod of
Milan in 390.

Meanwhile, in the East, Mary's virginity in childbearing is a
constantly recurring theme in the writings of Saint Ephrem of
Syria (d. 373), who taught the sublime truth that Emmanuel was
able to "open the womb" of Mary without violating her virginity.[22]

Saints Augustine and Jerome at the turn of the fourth century
also gave important testimony concerning the miraculous nature
of Christ's birth. Perhaps the most striking image is Saint
Augustine's parallel between the virgin birth and the post-
Resurrection appearance in which Jesus entered the room
despite locked doors (cf. Jn. 20:19), an image also employed by
Saint Ephrem.[23]

Pope St. Leo the Great, in his famous "Tome," provided the
following teaching concerning the virgin birth:

[19] Saint Ambrose, *Letter to Siricius, Bishop of Rome*, as translated in The Fathers of the
Church Series (New York: The Fathers of the Church, Inc., 1954), vol. 26, 225-30.
[20] Cf. Catechism, no. 724. See also Tim Gray, "What's in a Name?" *Lay Witness*
(December 1998), 12.
[21] See footnote no. 19, *supra*.
[22] Walter J. Burghardt, S.J., "Mary in Eastern Patristic Thought," as reproduced in Carol,
ed., *Mariology*, vol. 2, 110.
[23] *Ibid.*

> [Jesus] was born in a "new type of birth" in that undefiled virginity experienced no concupiscence, yet supplied the material for the flesh. . . . [T]he Lord Jesus Christ, born from a virgin's womb, does not have a nature different from ours just because His birth was an unusual one.[24]

This remarkable document was read to the assembly at the Council of Chalcedon in 451, at which it was adopted unconditionally and enthusiastically, thereby reflecting both Western and Eastern acceptance of this teaching.

Further corroboration may be found in the above-quoted canon from the Lateran Council of 649, which referred to Mary's giving birth to Jesus "without loss of integrity." This canon was approved by Pope St. Martin I and eventually was adopted by Constantinople III in 681.

The dogma firmly in place, subsequent magisterial statements serve only as reaffirmations of this timeless truth. Most recently, at Vatican II, we have the following statement, which cites the Lateran Council and Pope St. Leo the Great:

> This union of the mother with the Son in the work of salvation is made manifest from the time of Christ's virginal conception up to his death . . . then also at the birth of Our Lord, who did not diminish his mother's virginal integrity but sanctified it (LG 57).

Virginity After the Birth of Christ

In one sense, Mary's virginity postpartum (after birth) is the easiest aspect of Mary's virginity to accept. After all, her giving birth to the Son of God without losing her virginity required a miracle, whereas her virginity thereafter, while granting the virgin birth, merely means that Mary remained a virgin—and consequently childless—for the rest of her earthly life.

---

[24] Letter no. 28, as translated in *St. Leo the Great: Letters*, The Fathers of the Church Series (New York: The Fathers of the Church, Inc., 1957), vol. 34, 97.

In another sense, Mary's virginity postpartum can be the most difficult to explain, because (1) those who would reduce divine Revelation to Scripture alone cannot find evidence to support this contention in the New Testament, and (2) there are New Testament passages that actually seem to contradict the Church's teaching. Without a proper understanding of the sources of Revelation, the first point cannot be overcome, because it is indeed true that an indisputable case for Mary's Perpetual Virginity cannot be made on Scripture alone. However, for the confused Catholic and curious Protestant alike, it is important to demonstrate that this Church teaching is not in conflict with the inspired text, lest Mary's Perpetual Virginity needlessly serve as a stumbling block for one who rightly venerates Sacred Scripture. In other words, it must be shown that Mary's virginity after giving birth to Christ—a teaching rooted in Tradition and proposed by the Magisterium—at minimum does not contradict the witness of Scripture. If this cannot be done satisfactorily, the Catholic view of divine Revelation lacks plausibility.

Mary's virginity postpartum, while not explicitly taught in Scripture,[25] is repeatedly attested by the Latin, Greek, and Syriac Fathers.[26] Outstanding among the patristic sources is Saint Jerome's biting treatise *On the Perpetual Virginity of the Blessed Mary Against Helvidius* (383), which not only affirms the teaching, but specifically addresses the objections against Mary's virginity postpartum that are typically raised in Protestant circles even today.

The following statement comes from Pope St. Siricius (392), in the course of approving the refutation of a certain Bonosus, who had asserted that Mary had other children:

---

[25] Implicit references would include Luke 1:34-35, which implies that Mary had taken a perpetual vow of virginity—otherwise the exchange does not make sense—and John 19:26-27, which suggests that there were not other children to whom Mary could be entrusted.

[26] For a listing of patristic sources, see Garrigou-Lagrange, *The Mother of the Savior and Our Interior Life*, 124.

> Surely, we cannot deny that regarding the sons of Mary the statement is justly censured, and your holiness has rightly abhorred it, that from the same virginal womb, from which according to the flesh Christ was born, another offspring was brought forth.[27]

The Second Council of Constantinople (553) gave Mary the title "*Aeiparthenos*" ("Ever-virgin"). The Lateran Council (649), approved by Pope St. Martin I and later accepted at Constantinople III (681), provided that "after [Christ's] birth [Mary] preserved her virginity inviolate."[28] This dogmatic truth has been reaffirmed repeatedly throughout the centuries, including in our era at Vatican II (cf. LG 52).

Perhaps the most persistent objection to Mary's virginity post-partum is the frequent scriptural reference to Jesus' "brothers" (e.g., Mt. 13:55; Mk. 3:31-35; Lk. 8:20; Jn. 2:12; 7:3-5; Acts 1:14; 1 Cor. 9:5; Gal. 1:19).[29] The fundamental response to this objection is that the Greek word *adelphos*, which is frequently translated "brother," can be used to designate not only a blood brother, but also other familial relationships.[30] *Adelphos* (or "brother"), standing alone, is thus inconclusive on the point. In fact, further examination of the texts alone reveals that at least some of these purported "brothers" were *not* the children of Mary.[31] Indeed, nowhere in Scripture is the Blessed Virgin Mary

---

[27] Henry Denzinger, *The Sources of Catholic Dogma*, trans. by Roy J. Deferrari (St. Louis: B. Herder Book Co., 1957), no. 91.

[28] As translated in Clarkson, *et al., The Church Teaches*, 204.

[29] For more in-depth treatment of this subject, see "Relative Obscurity: The 'Brothers and Sisters' of Jesus," a FAITH FACT published by Catholics United for the Faith, 827 N. Fourth St., Steubenville, OH 43952, (800) 693-2484, www.cuf.org, and sources cited therein.

[30] Cf. Saint Jerome, *On The Perpetual Virginity of the Blessed Mary Against Helvidius*, as translated in The Fathers of the Church Series (Washington: Catholic University of America Press, Inc., 1965), vol. 53, 3-43. Saint Jerome teaches that individuals are called "brothers" in Scripture for four reasons: birth, race, kinship, and affection. He also cites the usual Scripture passages that demonstrate the wider use of "brother" (e.g., Gen. 13:8; 29:10-15).

[31] Donnelly, "The Perpetual Virginity of the Mother God," 247-50; Saint Jerome, *ibid.*, 28-30.

ever identified as the mother of anyone other than Jesus. In addition, the brothers appear to be older than Jesus, and there is ample scriptural support for the proposition that Mary had no children *before* Jesus (e.g., Mt. 1:18-25; Lk. 1:26-38; 2:7).

Another objection is the reference to Christ's being a "first-born" son in Luke 2:7, which some may see as implying that there were other sons. Saint Jerome convincingly refuted this objection over 1,500 years ago:

> Every only child is a first-born child; but not every first-born is an only child. A first-born child is not only one after whom other children are also born, but also one before whom no other child is born.[32]

Saint Jerome went on to point out that the Jewish practice was to offer sacrifice upon the birth of a "first-born," without the necessity of waiting for subsequent children to be born.[33] Fr. Brown lends further support, explaining that *prototokos* ("first-born") only means no prior child, and is sometimes the equivalent of *monogenes* ("only born").[34]

Similar analysis can be used to dispel the inference drawn from Matthew 1:18-25 that Joseph and Mary had relations *after* the birth of Jesus. The passage refers to the time *before* Joseph and Mary lived together and to their not having relations "*until* she had borne a son." This passage merely asserts that up to a definite point in time the marriage was not consummated, but does not speak to the issue of consummation after Jesus' birth.

This sort of discourse was not uncommon during biblical times. For example, we find this "until" clause in 2 Samuel 6:23: "And Michal the daughter of Saul had no child [until] the day of

---

[32] *On the Perpetual Virginity of the Blessed Mary Against Helvidius*, 23.

[33] *Ibid.*, 23-25. For example, Exodus 13:1-2 provides, "The LORD said to Moses, 'Consecrate to me all the first-born; whatever is the first to open the womb among the people of Israel, both of man and of beast, is mine.'"

[34] Brown, *The Birth of the Messiah*, 398.

her death."[35] Clearly, Michal did not have children *after* she died either! Saint Jerome identified several similar passages, including Genesis 35:4; Deuteronomy 34:5-6; Psalm 123:2; Isaiah 46:4; Matthew 28:20; and 1 Corinthians 15:23-26.[36]

The fourth major objection is based on an inability to reconcile postpartum virginity with Joseph and Mary's having a "true marriage."[37] Marriage involves a mutual, unconditional gift of self that may be physically expressed, but not necessarily. One may possess a right without its exercise. Consent, not consummation, is "the indispensable element that 'makes the marriage'" (Catechism, no. 1626). Pope John Paul II has reaffirmed that Joseph and Mary had a true marriage.[38]

New Creation

It is critical to understand Marian doctrines in light of the mystery of Christ (Eph. 3:4, 11) and in light of the unfolding of God's plan in the fullness of time (Gal. 4:4-5). The special favors granted to the Mother of God—including permitting a creature's voluntary participation in the "new creation" to be, in a sense, necessary—are a mystery of God's loving providence rather than the inevitable result of reasoning syllogistically with the data of divine Revelation. The meaning of the announcement of the angel Gabriel to Mary concerning the virginal conception (Lk. 1:35) is well summarized by Cardinal Ratzinger:

---

[35] Some modern translations use "to" or "till" instead of "until," but the sense is the same. Check your Bible and see. In addition, "He had not known her when she bore a son" (Knox translation) is a linguistically acceptable translation of Matthew 1:25. Another example is the use of "until" in the first paragraph of this chapter. Clearly the author is not implying that Mary lost her virginity *after* she was taken to heaven!

[36] *On the Perpetual Virginity of the Blessed Mary Against Helvidius*, 18-21.

[37] Cf. Mark Miravalle, *Introduction to Mary* (Santa Barbara, CA: Queenship Publishing Co., 1993), 163.

[38] Pope John Paul II, Apostolic Letter On the Person and Mission of St. Joseph in the Life of Christ and His Church *Redemptoris Custos* (1989), no. 7.

Our gaze is led beyond the covenant with Israel to the creation: In the Old Testament the Spirit of God is the power of creation; He it was who hovered over the waters in the beginning and shaped chaos into cosmos (Gen. 1:2); when He is sent, living beings are created (Ps. 104 [103]:30). So what is to happen here to Mary is a new creation: the God who called forth being out of nothing makes a new beginning amid humanity: his Word becomes flesh.[39]

Mary's Perpetual Virginity, then, not only exhorts us to imitate Mary's charity, discipleship, fidelity, and purity (cf. LG 63-64), but highlights the singularity of the Incarnation, of God's taking the initiative to recreate the human race through His Son, the New Adam, who was really "born of the Virgin Mary."[40]

We can no more deny the "physicality" of Mary's virginity any more than we can deny the physicality of Mary's motherhood. Mary's Perpetual Virginity points us unmistakably to the Christological mystery of the eternal Word's becoming flesh in Mary's womb, in the marriage—without commingling—of the human and divine through God's "marvellous condescension" (cf. DV 13).

Leon J. Suprenant, Jr. is the president of Catholics United for the Faith and the editor of Lay Witness, *a monthly magazine for lay Catholics. He received his law degree from the University of Missouri-Kansas City School of Law and his master's degree in theology from Franciscan University of Steubenville. He is the coauthor of* FAITH FACTS: Answers to Catholic Questions *and general editor of* Servants of the Gospel *(Emmaus Road Publishing). He resides in Steubenville, Ohio, with his wife Maureen and their four daughters.*

---

[39] Cardinal Joseph Ratzinger, *Introduction to Christianity* (San Francisco: Ignatius Press, 1990), 206.

[40] *Ibid.*, 208-10; cf. Rom. 5:12-21; 1 Cor. 15:20 *et seq.* Jesus is not the Son of God by reason of the virginal conception, as though the Father supplied the Y chromosomes, but by reason of His eternal generation that enables Him to call God the Father "Abba."

CHAPTER VIII

Called to Be
Children of Mary
God's Family Plan

CURTIS MARTIN

As I began my way up the stairs, I felt my legs lock. It was not a muscle cramp or some other form of paralysis—it was fear that gripped me. I still remember my first visit several years ago to an AIDS hospice run by Mother Teresa's Missionaries of Charity. I was living with a wise and tireless priest in San Francisco. Part of our group's apostolate was to visit the patients in this hospice. It was my first visit, and I was surprised at my reaction.

At that time, we were not completely sure how AIDS was passed along, but we knew there was no cure. I knew that there were men only a few feet away from me who were dying from an incurable and contagious disease, and something deep within me did not want to go upstairs. I said a brief prayer and began my way up the stairway. It was an awe-inspiring sight to see the complete and total Christ-like service that the nuns provided to these poor dying men. I began to work through my initial awkwardness and asked the Holy Spirit to help me overcome my fear. I still remember my few visits to this hospice and the intense conversations I was able to have with these men. It is amazing how when you are confronted with death, you do not feel the need for small talk.

My most memorable experience at the hospice occurred one evening when I was invited to hear a priest, Father Donald McGuire, S.J., give a talk to these men and the nuns who cared for them. As I sat in the room, Father McGuire began to speak directly to the men:

> None of you would be here tonight if your fathers had not fallen into one of these categories. They were either dead, drunk, drugged up, divorced, or somehow disabled from loving you the way they were intended to.

I thought to myself, "Father, what are you doing? We are in the middle of the gay district in San Francisco. How can you have the audacity to blame their circumstances on the lack of a father in their lives?" As my mind raced with all the responses of our politically correct society, I looked around the room. No one was arguing and, without exception, these dying men were beginning to weep. I realized that father was not speaking to gay activists. He was speaking to individual men who were experiencing the very real anguish of AIDS and preparing for their death.

As Father McGuire continued to speak to these men, he shared with them that each of us desires love and a sense of belonging. We were made that way by God. Our family is intended by God to be a place where we can find love and happiness and begin to discover God Himself. When we do not find love in our home, where we expect it to be, we often look for it in a world that offers only false options. These men knew, in a way that goes beyond all political arguments, that they would not have turned to lives of drug abuse or homosexuality if they had not fallen for the world's lie. As Saint Augustine says, "[Y]ou have made us for yourself, and our heart is restless until it rests in you" (as quoted in Catechism, no. 30). With tears running down their cheeks, these men continued to listen to Father McGuire:

> At the heart of the Gospel message is the heart of a loving Father crying out to His children, desiring to comfort them and provide them with the love He has created them for. At the

very end of Old Testament prophecy, Malachi states, "Behold, I will send you Elijah the prophet before the great and terrible day of the LORD comes. And he will turn the hearts of fathers to their children and the hearts of children to their fathers, lest I come and smite the land with a curse" (Mal. 4:5-6). These are the last words of prophecy in the Old Testament, and nothing more is heard for hundreds of years until John the Baptist comes on the scene in the spirit of Elijah preparing the way for Jesus Christ. At the heart of Jesus' Gospel is a call to receive His Heavenly Father as our own. In His greatest sermon, the Sermon on the Mount, Jesus pours out His heart and speaks of His Heavenly Father. Sixteen times in the sermon He mentions Our Heavenly Father and teaches us to cry out to God not as some impersonal, all-powerful being, but rather with the words, "Our Father who art in heaven. . . ." The Gospel is intended by God to address the longings of our human hearts and it is never too late to repent, to turn our lives around and call upon the mercy of God and receive His forgiveness and love.

Most of us are not dying from AIDS, but in our hearts each of us knows that we are dying to be loved. In this chapter we will discover how God has placed the desire for love in our hearts and how His plan includes a family where we will discover and grow in His love both in this life and in the life to come.

Personal Relationship

Our Evangelical brothers and sisters have tapped into the depth of our hunger for love and happiness. When they ask, "Do you have a personal relationship with Jesus Christ?" it seems to touch a nerve. Often Catholics are put off by this question, and yet we need to realize that a personal relationship with Jesus Christ is every bit as much a Catholic issue as it is a Protestant issue, because it is profoundly a human issue. Every follower of Christ is called to a deep and personal relationship with our living Savior. Catholics frequently miss the boat when this question is asked. The typical response to the question is "Yes, I'm a Catholic." This answer may show a lack of understanding for the question. It is as if someone asked, "Do you know the President of the United States?" and I replied, "Yes, I am an American."

As Catholics, we are members of God's family, but do we really know Him? We seem to have things backwards these days, as if membership in the Church were the fundamental issue. In reality, our membership in the Church is the primary result of our relationship with Jesus Christ.

But not only Catholics miss the point here. Our Evangelical brothers and sisters frequently miss the depth and intensity of the relationship Christ offers. We could ask, "Do you have a personal relationship with Jesus Christ?" and they might respond, "Yes, He is my Lord and Savior." This is true as far as it goes, but the Gospel actually provides much more. As Christians we have been called to have a personal relationship with Jesus Christ, but we need to understand the nature of this relationship. I have a personal relationship with my next-door neighbor. His children are friends of my children, and his wife is a friend of my wife. But Christ is not calling us to be merely His friends.

I also have a personal relationship with my wife. This is very different. The relationship I have with my wife is so profound that she is not only my friend, but also part of my family. In fact, her family has become my family as well. And this is much more intense. Because of the covenant of marriage, I am called to an intimate relationship with people with whom I may have very little in common, except for our mutual love of my wife.

Just as my personal relationship with my wife has consequences, so too does our personal relationship with Christ. We see this in the Gospel, as Jesus not only reveals His Heavenly Father, but also invites us to accept God as Our Heavenly Father. He comes to us as our brother. In fact, the Hebrew word for redeemer, *go-el*, literally means "kinsman redeemer." This is the heart of the Incarnation. The eternal Son of God becomes a son of Adam. Jesus' favorite title for Himself is Son of man, literally *ben adam* (son of Adam). Jesus refers to Himself as Son of man more than any other title in Scripture, and yet no one else ever refers to him as Son of man. He wants us to understand that, in the flesh, He has become one with us so that He might be our kinsman and redeem us back into a deep personal and familial relationship with His Heavenly Father. In fact, an accurate summary of salvation history is that Our Heavenly Father is taking the wounded, fractured family of humanity and reconstituting it *in* Christ into the Family of God. Yes, as Catholic Christians we do have a personal relationship with Jesus Christ—He is our first-born brother, His Father is our Father, and His brothers and sisters become our brothers and sisters. And His mother is also our mother.

What Must We Do to Be Saved?

You may have had someone ask you whether or not you are saved. It is an interesting question when you think about it. We often find ourselves focusing on what we have been saved *from*—from sin and death, the punishment due to sin. Though a question still remains: If that is what we are saved *from*, what are we saved *for*? If we are going to present the Gospel in its entirety, we need to share not only what we are saved *from*, but also what we are saved *for*.

Early converts to the faith had this same question. After Saint Peter preached to a multitude on Pentecost Sunday, the converts were moved by faith and, in their desire to accept Christ, they turned to Peter and asked, "Brethren, what shall we do?" Peter said to them, "Repent, and be baptized every one of you in the name of Jesus Christ for the forgiveness of your sins; and you shall receive the gift of the Holy Spirit" (Acts 2:37-38). Saint Peter's response is twofold: We need to reform our lives and be baptized.

To repent means to turn around and go the other direction. Prior to our acceptance of Christ and coming to receive Him, each of us has lived a self-willed life. We have chosen our own way and that must end. Now we accept the lordship of Jesus Christ and He leads us into the joy of salvation—into His family.

Jesus gives us two examples of how this self-willed life may manifest itself in the parable of the prodigal son (cf. Lk. 15:11-32). In the first case we have the prodigal, whose willfulness had caused him to reject his father's love, seek his share of the inheritance, and depart from his father's home to waste his wealth on sinful living. After spending his inheritance, he found himself alone in his misery and decided to return to his father's house, even if only as a slave. While still a great distance away, his father saw him and ran to meet him and received him back with rejoicing, as a son who had been dead and was alive again. Many of us have allowed our self-willed life to lead us far from Christ into a life of sin. We have experienced the reality that pursuing happiness apart from God's will leads only to misery. God is calling each of us to turn our lives around and receive our Father's love and forgiveness.

The parable does not end there. The father has a second son. This older son is filled with anger when he sees his father rejoicing at the return of his wayward son. "Lo, these many years I have served you" (Lk. 15:29), he says. His word for "serve" literally means to be a slave. This son has been loyal and has done what his father told him, but he has done it in the spirit of slavery rather than in the spirit of sonship. His father's response is telling: "Son, you are always with me, and all that is mine is yours" (Lk. 15:31).

While many of us have strayed far from God in our actions, others of us have strayed from Him in our hearts. We have tried to be good and play by the rules. We have gone to church, but we have done so out of a sense of obligation rather than love. Whether we have rebelled against our Father or simply treated Him as our Master rather than our Dad, God is calling each of us to repent—to return to His fatherly love. This is the first part of Saint Peter's response, "Repent, and be baptized" (Acts 2:38). Repentance makes it possible for us to be reconciled to God; Baptism—or Confession for those who have fallen after Baptism—opens the door to God's life and love within our soul.

Jesus saved us from our sin and from death, which is its consequence. As Saint Peter says, we have been "called . . . out of darkness into his marvelous light" (1 Pet. 2:9). However, the question remains, "If we have been saved out of these things, what have we been saved into?" Scripture teaches us that our salvation is not simply some external declaration, as if we have been given

some clean clothes but are still the same filthy people we were
before Christ had redeemed us. Saint Paul teaches, "Therefore,
if any one is in Christ, he is in a new creation; the old has
passed away, behold, the new has come" (2 Cor. 5:17). This is
a fascinating aspect of the Gospel of Jesus Christ. Our salvation
is not an external mechanism; Christ's work is internal and runs
to the very core and fiber of our being. We are new creations in
Christ. Saint Peter teaches:

> [H]e has granted to us his precious and very great promises,
> that through these you may escape from the corruption that is
> in the world because of passion, and become partakers of the
> divine nature (2 Pet. 1:4).

God gives us the free and undeserved gift of His grace
through which we may be justified. Saint John says, "But to all
who received him, who believed in his name, he gave power to
become children of God" (Jn. 1:12). As this belief leads us to
repentance and Baptism (cf. Acts 2:38), we are united to Christ
and His new life is born within us. Saint Paul teaches:

> Do you not know that all of us who have been baptized into
> Christ Jesus were baptized into his death? We were buried
> therefore with him by baptism into death, so that as Christ was
> raised from the dead by the glory of the Father, we too might
> walk in newness of life (Rom. 6:3-4).

This language appears a bit strange. We are not baptized *by*
Christ; we are baptized *into* Christ. What does it mean to be *in*
Christ? Saint Paul stresses this point. We are not only following
Christ, but we are *in* Christ. At least sixty-five times in his epistles,
Saint Paul refers to Christians as being *in* Christ. Saint Paul says we
have been baptized into Christ Jesus. He says Christ enters us: "I
have been crucified with Christ; it is no longer I who live, but
Christ who lives in me" (Gal. 2:20). Indeed, as we discover
what Christ has saved us *for*, what He saved us *from* almost
pales in comparison. Saint Paul reminds us, "Do you not know

that you are God's temple and that God's Spirit dwells in you?" (1 Cor. 3:16). We have become children of God in a way that transcends our nature, our understanding, and even our imagination (cf. 1 Cor. 2:9; 1 Jn. 3:2).

God is pure spirit and infinitely perfect. His nature is different from ours. We may be tempted to think that when He speaks of us as members of the family, it is a metaphor in the same way that I would speak of my dog being a member of our family. Shannon shares in the scraps from our table and the overflow of the love from my wife and children, but she in no way, shape, or form is a true member of our family. However, once we are baptized into Christ we have become God's children. Scripture says, "See what love the Father has given us, that we should be called children of God; and so we are" (1 Jn. 3:1). The miracle of the Incarnation makes this possible.

In Jesus Christ, God not only offers a solution and satisfaction for our sin, He draws us into His very life.

> But when the time had fully come, God sent forth his Son, born of woman, born under the law, to redeem those who were under the law, so that we might receive adoption as sons (Gal. 4:4-5).

In Christ, God has united Himself to humanity, and what God has joined, no man can put asunder (cf. Mt. 19:6).

A Sign of Contradiction

Such is the power and the intensity of the Gospel of Jesus Christ, that we are now children of God. But this "Good News" is a scandal to the world. The prophet Simeon warned that Jesus would be a sign of contradiction appointed for the rise and fall of many (cf. Lk. 2:34). At the time of Christ, there were many who thought they believed in God and wanted to follow Him, but Christ literally offered His flesh as a challenge. In effect, He asked, "If you believe in God, will you follow Me?" Many could not follow Him, and their faith was proved to be lacking.

In the beginning, God created man in His image, and it has been said that for the rest of history, man has tried to recreate God in his image. It is scandalous that the God of the universe, Creator of the world, the all-powerful, the all-knowing would take flesh in a stable in Bethlehem and call the entire world to follow Him. "I am the way, and the truth, and the life; no one comes to the Father, but by me" (Jn. 14:6). The scandal of Jesus continues today. If we accept Jesus Christ, we must accept His family, the Church.

The Family: God's First Icon

Within the rich heritage of Christianity, one of the most beautiful forms of sacred art is the icon. In icons we see Our Lord, the Blessed Virgin Mary, and other saints depicted in a manner which calls us to ponder the sacred mysteries they represent. As I sit in my office, I look at a wonderful picture of my family. The pictures are not only a representation of the love that I have for them; they are also a reminder. But an icon is far more than a picture. Icons are sacred and mysterious images which lead us into prayer and into pondering the Person, the work, and the life and death of Christ. They are images that reveal far more than words can describe. According to Scripture, God Himself made the first icon or image of Himself:

> Then God said, "Let us make man in our image, after our likeness; and let them have dominion. . . ." So God created man in his own image, in the image of God he created him; male and female he created them (Gen. 1:26-27).

After God had created man, male and female, He blessed them and gave them a command saying, "Be fruitful and multiply" (Gen. 1:28).

From the beginning, humanity was created in the image of God. We are created in a community of persons and called to fruitful love. When God sought to re-create humanity in Christ, He did not depart from His original plan, but rather reconstituted the family of man into the Family of God. Our first parents, Adam and Eve, refused to love God as they were called to, and fell. We as Christians have had our hearts renewed in Christ and He invites us into His family through adoption as sons and daughters of God. Jesus, our brother, "the first-born among many brethren" (Rom. 8:29), has come and brought us back to God the Father.

God's Holy Family

Because God's plan of salvation brings us into His family, Mary's role is significant to all of us. Just as the eternal Son of God has but one Father, and He has shared His Father with us, so too, through the Incarnation, God's Son has been born of one woman and His mother becomes the mother of all Christians in the life of grace. As beloved disciples, we are called to live our life within the Family of God not only by receiving Jesus' Father, but also by following the beloved disciple John's example and taking His mother into our home. "Then he said to the disciple, 'Behold, your mother!' And from that hour the disciple took her to his own home" (Jn. 19:27).

Jesus, the eternal Son of God, was a faithful Jew. He was bound by the Fourth Commandment to honor both His Father, God, and His mother, Mary. The Hebrew word for honor literally means "to glorify." We are Christians precisely because we are brought *into* Christ, and He continues in us to honor His Heavenly Father. Certainly He would not cease to honor His mother. The role of Mary in the Gospel is to be understood in light of her motherhood. Honoring Mary is not the product of excessive religious sentimentality; it is the very practical consequence of being part of the Family of God. As Saint Paul has already reminded us, "when the time had fully come, God sent forth his Son, born of woman" (Gal. 4:4). If we read on in Galatians, we see that the effect of Christ's being born of Mary is that we are adopted into His family.

At times, Catholics and Eastern Orthodox Christians have been accused of making too much of Mary. This is a failure to

understand history. The teachings about Mary have always been
a simple reflection of the Incarnation of the eternal Son of God
as her Son. In 431, the Church declared definitively that Mary
was *Theotokos*, the God-bearer or Mother of God. This was not
done primarily to honor Mary, but to clarify orthodox Christian
teaching against those who were denying that Jesus Christ was
truly God. By affirming the fact that Mary was the Mother of
God, the Church affirmed that Jesus was truly God. So it is with
all the teachings concerning Mary. Under the inspiration of the
Holy Spirit, Mary herself teaches:

> My soul magnifies the Lord, and my spirit rejoices in God my
> Savior, for he has regarded the low estate of his handmaiden.
> For behold, henceforth all generations will call me blessed
> (Lk. 1:46-48).

Mary is, by her nature, a lowly handmaid but, by the grace of
God, her soul magnifies the Lord, and she has become the
Mother of God and our mother too, if we live in Christ.

As Christians, the very spirit of Christ is alive within us. It
is our responsibility within the Family of God to honor Our
Heavenly Father and our spiritual mother. Mary's role as mother
and "the woman" is not insignificant to our salvation. As we
have seen in preceding chapters, those who keep the commandments of God and bear witness to Jesus are children of
Mary (cf. Rev. 12:17).

To live in Christ, we must love what He loves and hate what
He hates. We know that the historical Jesus had a historical
mother, Mary, and that He loved her. He honored His mother and
He continues to honor and glorify her *in* us. Marian devotion is
therefore not an option for the Christian, but an obligation in
keeping with the Fourth Commandment. If we are to have God
as Father in Christ, we must have Mary as mother. If we are to
have a personal relationship with Christ, it must be within His
family. He has left us no other options. It is not as though we can
choose another way to be saved. We have to accept the only way

He has provided for us. Because Christ is alive in us, the Church is an extension of His Incarnation and the Church is the universal Family of God. If the essence of salvation, as Scripture teaches, is divine sonship, then to speak of salvation outside of God's family is to misunderstand things completely. Being outside of God's family is precisely what we need to be saved from.[1]

The Challenge of Family Life

The Body of Christ, the Church, challenges us to be in relationship with the Jesus of history. As C.S. Lewis points out, there is a real danger that we exchange faith in the true God for one of our own imagination.[2] This may occur more easily than we might think. We all have an image of what Jesus must have been like— His mannerisms, the tone of His voice, how He smiled, and so forth. We ought to base this image on the truth. What if my image of Jesus only focuses on the "nice" things He had to say? How do I deal with the real Jesus who calls the Pharisees a brood of vipers or sons of hell? If the Catholic Church is the covenant family Christ has established, is any of us free to accept His covenant and yet not accept the family which that covenant created?

It is easy to have a personal relationship with Christ if He is a figment of our imagination and not a historical figure who established a Church, a family, in history, in time. If we are going to yield our lives to Christ, we must accept His forgiveness and be reconciled as sons and daughters, or we will not be reconciled at all. Some will say, "I love Jesus, I just don't have any use for the Church." Given the clear teaching of Scripture, this is nonsense. How can someone say, "I accept the king but I have no use for his kingdom"? It is almost impossible for me to imagine having a close friend who has no use for my wife or my children, and this

---

[1] Cf. Scott Hahn, "The Mystery of the Family of God," as published in Hahn and Suprenant, eds., *Catholic for a Reason: Scripture and the Mystery of the Family of God* (Steubenville, OH: Emmaus Road Publishing, 1998), 11.

[2] Cf. C.S. Lewis, *Mere Christianity* (New York: Macmillan Publishing Co., 1952), 111.

is just a friend! What if one of my sons were to say, "Dad, I love you, but I really don't have much use for Mom and my brothers and sisters"? As we have seen, we are more than friends of God. We are His family. Just as Mary gave the Word flesh in her womb, she puts flesh on the Gospel today. She requires us to relate to the historical Jesus, to whom she gave birth and who founded the Catholic Church, which is the universal Family of God.

When we speak about the importance of being a member of the Church, it is not as if we need to join a club or organization to be saved. But we must realize that if we are going to allow God to save us, He is going to save us as a Father and call us into His family. Our devotion to the Blessed Virgin Mary flows from the "family Spirit" our salvation has given us. The Spirit of God has been given to us so that we might cry out, "Abba, Father!" (Rom. 8:15). So too, that same Spirit will give us tenderness toward our spiritual mother. Just as Simeon the prophet, under the inspiration of the Holy Spirit, predicted that Jesus would be a sign of contradiction, he also turned to Mary and said, "[A] sword will pierce through your own soul also, that thoughts out of many hearts may be revealed" (Lk. 2:35). Our childlike love for Mary reveals that our hearts are those of true children of God. Our desire to honor our mother is a manifestation of our divine sonship. If we lack this tender affection for our mother, in what way can we see ourselves possessing the Spirit of God?

Call to Conversion

God our Father has created us for Himself. Because of this, each of us has a deep desire for love and happiness. However, each of us has also been broken by sin. As Isaiah the prophet says, "All we like sheep have gone astray; we have turned every one to his own way" (Is. 53:6). Because of sin, we find ourselves searching for love and happiness apart from the will of God. In Christ, God has reconciled the world to Himself. Jesus has provided the one means for our salvation. The eternal Son of God became man and won for the sons and daughters of man the privilege of becoming sons and daughters of God. Our salvation is a free and undeserved gift by which we are invited to become children of the Heavenly Father and accept Jesus as the absolute Lord of our lives.

God the Father welcomes us into His kingdom. Christ's brothers and sisters become ours and His mother becomes our mother. Just as faith allows us to see that Jesus is no ordinary man but the true Son of God, so too, we begin to see that the Church is no ordinary institution, but God's own family. This family is open to anyone who will yield to Christ and, by doing so, God will gather all of us together in accordance with His eternal purpose (cf. Eph. 3:11). Scripture teaches that in God's family there will be

> one body and one Spirit, just as you were called to the one hope that belongs to your call, one Lord, one faith, one baptism, one God and Father of us all, who is above all and through all and in all (Eph. 4:4-6).

As we abide in Christ, we will continue to abide in His family, the Church. Within the Family of God, we will find that God satisfies our longings for love and happiness. Draw close to Christ, and He will draw you close to His Father and His mother, and they will draw us close to one another, and the world will know that we are the disciples of Christ because of the love we have for one another (cf. Jn. 13:35).

CHAPTER IX

Mary,
Full of Grace

KIMBERLY HAHN

Of all of the obstacles littering my path toward the Catholic Church, none loomed larger than Mary. She represented diversion from true devotion to Our Lord to a plastic (or ceramic or marble) substitute. She was only the box that held the Present; did it honor the Giver to play with the box and ignore the Gift? Depending on which Catholic friend I spoke to, I heard qualities attributed to her that bordered on divinity, including titles such as Queen of Heaven and Mother of God. How could I reconcile the love for Jesus which I shared in common with Catholic brothers and sisters with the antagonism I felt toward Mary, His mother?

As my husband Scott shared his growing appreciation for the virgin mother of Jesus, I felt challenged to examine her role for the first time, apart from a prejudice against Catholic practices I did not understand. There had been a subconscious exclusion of Mary from my life of faith (except for a statue in the crèche my mother displayed at Christmas). Now I began an examination of the passages in Scripture describing Mary. Who was she? What did she do?

Fact: Mary was a young virgin, from David's royal line, who loved God and wanted to serve Him faithfully.

Fact: God chose Mary to be the mother of His Son so that He would be her Savior and ours.

Fact: Mary responded "YES!" with her whole heart. She was willing to do the Father's will, no matter the cost.

Fact: By the power of the Holy Spirit, the Second Person of the Godhead, the Son, took on human flesh within the womb of Mary, thereby becoming her Son as well as God's Son. She was the channel through whom Jesus received human nature. And Jesus, as Son of God (fully God) *and* Son of Mary (fully man), was able to save us from sin.

Never before had I acknowledged Mary as my primary role model. Now I could see she had done what I wanted to do: respond immediately to God's call. I had a new appreciation for the gift of this virgin's "yes" to God—the gift of Jesus through her to me. Even so, I did not want to examine or come to terms with the claims of the Catholic Church about her. Not yet.

Scott, on the other hand, was reading widely in Catholic theology and beginning to practice some Catholic devotions, including the Rosary. Unbeknownst to me, he had "put God to the test" with the Rosary and believed the answered prayer should be shared with me. He spoke with enthusiasm; I could barely respond. I did not even know he had a rosary, let alone used it!

In the ensuing months, our conversations ranged from theological discussions to heated debates. Scott would approach me to read from an article or book only to find me either less than enthusiastic or downright hostile. "If it's about Mary, I don't want to hear it!" was my frequent response.

Sometimes Scott, knowing the discussion would go no further, would head out the door. The jingling sound of beads alerted me that he was on his way to pray, to take a walk with Mary. How I resented that! No matter what she was in this life, I believed in heaven she was perfectly sweet, kind, and gentle (hardly the picture of me at the time!), and he would receive consolation from her that I could not give. So, not only did I struggle with Mary theologically, but I also struggled with jealousy toward her.

One day, following just such a departure, I went into our bedroom, my heart aching. There on Scott's dresser I saw a pamphlet on the Rosary—what idolatrous propaganda! More to prove my point than out of curiosity, I thought I would just take a peek.

I was amazed. The booklet began with the Apostles' Creed, a creed I said regularly. Next, it listed the Lord's Prayer (or Our Father), a prayer I had studied and prayed all of my life. Skipping over the "Hail Mary" for the moment, I glanced at the final prayer, the Doxology (or Glory Be)—again an exclamation of praise I had prayed and sung frequently since childhood. And the booklet offered meditations on the basic mysteries of the Christian faith—all of which were biblical (except for the last two, I thought). I looked more closely—there was less here to be offended by than I had previously thought.

Now for the "Hail Mary"—that was off base, wasn't it? Certainly asking the dead to pray went beyond the bounds of Christian devotion. I was unwilling to ask why Catholics prayed this ancient, repetitive prayer to Mary, though I had to admit that one glance at the booklet revealed my own misunderstanding. The Rosary was not nearly as offensive as I had thought. And when I was willing to examine it more fully, I just might come to a different conclusion from what I currently held. I shelved a study of this Marian devotion until later.

Much to my dismay, Scott was received into the Catholic Church in Milwaukee, Wisconsin, at the Easter Vigil, 1986. I felt abandoned by him and, in many ways, by God Himself. I felt very isolated, not knowing how to share my struggle with friends and family whose sympathy might end up being a cause of division between Scott and me. And I did not want to reveal my pain to Catholic friends who could not relate to it. I held onto threads of faith, writing in my prayer journal, "O God, to whom can I go? And don't tell me Mary and the saints!"

For more details, I refer readers to Scott's and my account of our journey of faith in *Rome Sweet Home* (Ignatius Press, 1994).

Many issues had to be examined, such as justification, Baptism, and the number and meaning of sacraments. Mary was only one hurdle among many; but for me she was undoubtedly the most difficult. Mary always loomed large as an unknowable and unsolvable mystery. How could I reconcile my heart to the Church's teaching on her when I resented so deeply the Church's emphasis on her?

One day I finally realized I had never asked God what *He* thought of Mary. He spoke to my heart some of the beautiful titles from Scripture that I only later discovered were part of the Litany of the Blessed Virgin Mary. In my journal I wrote, "pure vessel, Ark of the Covenant, and beloved daughter." God beckoned to me to follow Him, looking at Mary from His perspective.

I discovered that the Catholic Church taught that Mary was only a creature; however, she *was* the only mother whose Son created her. She was sinless because her Son saved her from sin from the moment of her conception. Just as God has saved us from committing various sins by saving us before we were tempted, so He saved Mary from committing any sins by saving her first. Mary's gift of sinlessness was not a matter of pride for her, but one of deep humility. She owed her entire salvation, as we do, to the mercy of God. She did not exalt herself; rather, the Lord is the One who exalted her for our benefit.

This study helped me to acknowledge Mary's role in salvation more deeply, and to peer into the mystery that she was my own spiritual mother and the spiritual mother of my children. I exchanged the bitterness in my heart towards her with the beginnings of love and gratitude for her.

Is the "Hail Mary" Biblical?

First, I examined the "Hail Mary" to see if it was biblical. "Hail Mary" is the angel Gabriel's greeting to the young virgin named Mary. He is communicating joy, just as the angels later tell the shepherds, "I bring you good news of a great joy" (Lk. 2:10).

Next, "full of grace" is a better translation of the Greek than "highly favored one." She *is* highly favored because she is *full* of grace. Gabriel, coming from God's throne, declares not how men see her but how God sees her: *full* of grace. It is not unusual for an angel to declare a quality which someone has; it *is* unusual that anyone would be called "full of grace."

What does this title mean? It means that God the Father has filled Mary with grace—His own divine life—so that she can be the mother of Jesus. This grace is given by the Father, through the Son, so that she can respond in obedience to the will of God by the power of the Holy Spirit. Consequently, by God's grace, she is full of grace; by grace, she is without sin.

"The Lord is with you" is a phrase used elsewhere by angels when someone is receiving a special call from God. Gabriel is telling Mary that the Lord is empowering her to do what He is asking her to do (cf. Catechism, no. 2676).

The next phrase comes from Elizabeth's greeting to Mary, "Blessed are you among women and blessed is the fruit of your womb." Mary echoes this statement in the Magnificat when she exclaims that future generations will call her blessed. I always thought, "Of course, she's blessed—no one else got to be the mother of the Savior of the world!" Now, as I studied this passage further, I saw that this blessing, recognized by future generations, is a declaration of the grace of God in her rather than a statement of good fortune from a human perspective. Not only was she given a gift in Jesus, she *is* a gift—most blessed among women. And this blessing is exemplified by and intensified through her faith-filled obedience.

Objectively, Mary is blessed by God in preparation for her call to bear the Savior of the world. Mary knew of other women in Israel's history who were honored above women in their time, such as Deborah's praise of Jael (Judg. 5:24) or the people's praise of Judith (Jud. 13:18). However, she is more blessed than these women because her call is a higher call.

Elizabeth uses the same term "blessed" for both Mary and Jesus. By blessing the fruit of Mary's womb and referring to Mary as "the mother of my Lord," Elizabeth acknowledges the presence of Jesus, though He would have been only a couple of weeks in gestation, at most. She acknowledges, in humility, that she is blessed by this visitation.

Later, in response to the honor given to Mary by followers of Jesus for physically bearing Jesus (Lk. 11:27-28), Jesus clarifies that her *greater* worthiness of honor resides in her immediate and ongoing response of obedience to God's call. Jesus does not imply that Mary's motherhood was unimportant (as I had previously thought); rather, He emphasizes her worthiness of praise lies in her faith and obedience—qualities His true disciples reflect.

The phrase "Holy Mary" is not found in Scripture. However, all believers are called to be holy as Our Heavenly Father is holy. Holy refers to someone or something being specially set apart by God. Holy also means "without sin," as are all those who enjoy heaven with Our Lord.

The next phrase, "Mother of God," was one of the most difficult for me to comprehend. I first heard this phrase in my systematic theology class at Gordon-Conwell Theological Seminary from a Baptist professor, Dr. Roger Nicole. I could not believe my ears! Was he saying Mary created God? (This is a common misconception of Protestants when the title "Mother of God" is used.)

When I approached Dr. Nicole, he addressed my concern. In a sense, the phrase says more about Jesus than about Mary. Jesus was fully God and fully man, two natures in the Second Person of the Godhead. When the Son of God took on human flesh from Mary, He really became the Son of Mary as well as the Son of God. When Mary became His mother, she was the mother of Jesus, the Second Person of the Trinity. Since Jesus is God the Son, we can properly say she is the Mother of God. To deny this, Dr. Nicole convinced me, is to deny that Jesus really is both fully man and fully God. And unless He is both fully God and fully man, He cannot be our Savior.

We read in Matthew 1:22-23:

> All this took place to fulfil what the Lord had spoken through the prophet: "Behold, a virgin shall conceive and bear a son, and his name shall be called Emmanu-el" (which means, God with us).

Mary did not create God, nor is she divine. However, she really is the mother of Jesus, and since Jesus is God, she is properly called the Mother of God.

Now came the most difficult part for me. To ask Mary to "Pray for us sinners now" was a red flag. The Old Testament clearly condemned contacting the dead as a form of witchcraft. Besides, those in heaven are so caught up with the Lord, they aren't paying attention to those of us here on earth. Why would they? Contacting them, even for prayer, seemed pointless.

At least I thought so until January 1989. After I hemorrhaged internally for three days, we discovered I had a tubal pregnancy. Following the surgery, Scott stayed as long as he could before returning home to our three small children, and I was left alone to cope with the pain—physical and emotional.

While I lay there, feeling empty and lonely, the Lord brought to mind a Scripture I had memorized long before, Hebrews 12:1-2:

> Therefore, since we are surrounded by so great a cloud of witnesses, let us also lay aside every weight, and sin which clings so closely, and let us run with perseverance the race that is set before us, looking to Jesus the pioneer and perfecter of our faith, who for the joy that was set before him endured the cross, despising the shame, and is seated at the right hand of the throne of God.

As I reviewed these verses, the Lord spoke to my heart of the reality of the communion of saints in a way I had never even considered before. First, the cloud of witnesses are the dead in Christ who, in fact, are more alive than we are. They surround us right now as witnesses to their own faithfulness to the Lord and to witness our faithfulness to the Lord. They are not waiting to condemn us for our failures, but cheering us on, aware of the challenges we face, and interceding on our behalf.

The Old Testament condemned contacting the dead to find out the future; it did not address requesting their prayers. If we are admonished throughout the New Testament to pray for one another as brothers and sisters in Christ, why would Christians pray less in heaven, where love is perfected? Prayer is the very breath of the soul—why would Christians pray less when they are in the presence of the One to whom they pray?

The last part of the "Hail Mary" is requesting prayer "at the hour of our death." We know we will need prayer when we are dying. Since we do not know when that time will come, we pray for that help now. It is a prayer for the grace of perseverance.

I did not learn this prayer in 1986 when I first read it. I learned it three years later in my son Michael's First Communion preparation class where I volunteered, partly to help out and partly to know what the Catholics were teaching my child. I learned the "Hail Mary," but I did not pray it until the evening of the children's First Penance service.

One of the little girls in the class returned to me in tears after her Confession. When I asked her why she was crying, she said, "He said to say the 'Hail Mary,' but I don't remember the words."

After a furtive glance to see if the teacher was nearby—she wasn't—I took a deep breath, tossed a prayer of apology to the Lord (hoping I wasn't sinning by saying this), and asked her to repeat after me, "Hail Mary, . . ." When we finished, she looked up at me and said, "Two times." So I took another deep breath, and repeated the prayer. You may not remember the first time you prayed the "Hail Mary," but I sure do.

I still was not open to praying the Rosary, though I had a better understanding of the communion of saints. I was uncomfortable about its repetitious nature and I did not understand how to meditate on the mysteries. Even though I was being received into the Church in ten days, when Scott asked me if I would like to learn how to pray the Rosary, my comment was, "I'm becoming a Catholic. Don't push it!" (What a docile response!)

He followed with an explanation. When he had visited EWTN, the vice president, Bill Stehltemeier, told him that the Holy Spirit had prompted him to give me his rosary. Scott told him I probably wouldn't be interested. Bill replied that the rosary had come from the Holy Father and he never thought he would part with it; but when the Holy Spirit prompted him to give it to me, he was going to obey.

When the rosary came in the mail, I knew I held a treasure, from a Catholic's perspective. What was I going to do with it? I picked up a little booklet on the scriptural Rosary that Scott previously had given me. With the rosary in the other hand, I prayed my first decade, hoping God would not be offended. The next day I prayed a second decade.

After the third day, I approached Scott and asked him for forgiveness for all of my willfulness. He also asked me to forgive him for the times he had confused the Holy Spirit's work in my life with his own role. We had many tears of joy and laughter.

One week later, my reception into the Catholic Church (Easter Vigil, 1990) was one more step toward embracing all of the treasures—including mother Mary—Jesus died for me to have. I continued to struggle with the repetitive nature of the Rosary (didn't Jesus condemn repetitive prayer as vain?) until I read an introduction to the Rosary by a nun. She asked the question, "How many times a day might a young child run to you and say, 'Mommy, I love you!'?" As a young mom I knew my children might tell me many times a day. Then she wrote, "Did you ever think of saying, 'Honey, that's just vain repetition!'? Of course not. The Rosary is an invitation to place our small hand in our mother's and say, 'Mommy, I love you, pray for me.'" Through this brief explanation, the Lord removed an obstacle for me. If I could just remember I was a small child in the faith, instead of an adult Christian, I could receive so much more of what the Lord wanted me to have.

In my first year as a Catholic, I felt prompted to prepare a Bible study on the mysteries of the Rosary, blending my knowledge of Scripture with this newfound relationship with my Lord's—and now my—mother. This study revealed wonderful insights for prayerful meditation of God's plan of salvation through Jesus and Mary.

I want to walk you briefly through each mystery, sharing a

few insights and demonstrating how I pray specifically for one of our children and godchildren with each mystery. I hope this enriches your own prayer life as it has mine and my family's.

First Joyful Mystery
The Annunciation
(Lk. 1:26-38)

Mary responds to the angel's greeting in true humility. God's plan is greater than any she could have imagined. To bear the Son of God and the Savior of the world was the desire of every Jewish girl—and this singular call was overwhelming. She knew the Scriptures and she knew how desperately her people and the whole world needed a Savior. Now God had chosen her, a humble maid, to give the Son of God flesh, to be His mother. Joy floods her heart.

Yet Mary asks, "How can this be?" She is not questioning the veracity of the angel's words like Zechariah had done regarding John the Baptist. Rather, she does not comprehend how God will do this—it's a statement of wonder.

Gabriel reveals God's plan. Just as the Holy Spirit overshadowed the ark of the covenant in the tabernacle and the Temple (Ex. 40:34-35), so will He will overshadow Mary, the new ark of the covenant. The old ark held the Word of God in stone tablets—the Ten Commandments; Mary will hold the living Word of God in her womb.

Mary's response to God's call is immediate and total: "Let it be to me according to your word." She freely cooperates in the work of salvation through her faith and obedience. She yields her whole self—mind, body, and will—to all of the joys and sorrows that are part of the mission the Lord is setting before her. She submits herself to the Person and work of her Savior.

My prayer (for at least one child and one godchild for each mystery):

> *Dear Lord, I know You have a mission these children. Please reveal Your plan for their lives in Your time. And please help*

them to respond in faithful obedience with their whole hearts
and wills, no matter what the cost, just as Mary did.

Second Joyful Mystery
The Visitation
(Lk. 1:39-56)

Mary is eager to bring Jesus to others. Mary shares her news
with Joseph whose incredulity leads to awkwardness and pain for
both. Leaving Joseph in God's hands, Mary goes immediately to
visit her cousin Elizabeth. She travels the arduous journey by
donkey (more than 150 miles from Nazareth to Ain Karim) to be
with Elizabeth, who is already in her sixth month of pregnancy
with John the Baptist. She has great news to share with someone
who also has wonderful news.

At Mary's greeting, Elizabeth is filled with the Holy Spirit
as is John the Baptist in her womb. Elizabeth proclaims, "And
why is this granted me, that the mother of my Lord should
come to me?" She testifies that Mary is the mother of the Savior
and that Jesus, small though He is, is the long-awaited Savior of
the world.

Mary's response in the Magnificat mirrors Hannah's song
of praise to God in 1 Samuel 2. She gives God all glory and
praise: "My soul magnifies the Lord, and my spirit rejoices in
God my Savior." God has chosen to elevate the humble, just as
He scatters the proud. Mary knows she is God's instrument to
glorify Him.

Mary acknowledges Jesus as her Savior—the only time a Son
has created His mother. She is God's masterpiece. Through her,
others will come to know the greatness of God's grace in her for
His plan of salvation. For this, all generations will call her
blessed. All Mary is and has is a gift from God.

My prayer:

Dear Lord, You want to do great things in and through these
children, if they will respond with humble hearts. Please give
them the joy and opportunity to take Jesus to others. And
please help them look for ways to serve rather than be served.

Third Joyful Mystery
The Nativity
(Lk. 2:1-20)

In God's perfect time—Saint Paul says the "fullness of time"—Mary delivers her precious baby in a cave-stable in Bethlehem. Mary and Joseph are the first to worship Jesus as God-man in the flesh. In the midst of their poverty, Jesus is *the* treasure. He offers Himself to Mary and Joseph; they respond by giving themselves to Him.

Jesus submits Himself to the littleness and powerlessness of infancy. In his commentary on the Gospel of Luke, Saint Ambrose writes:

> He made Himself a child . . . to enable you to become a perfect man; He was wrapped in swaddling clothes to free you from the bonds of death. . . . He came down on earth to enable you to rise up to heaven; He had no place in the inn so that you might have many mansions in heaven.

The shepherds go in haste after the angel's message because they believe God's Word, just as Mary had gone in haste to Elizabeth following the angel's message. Theirs was not a half-hearted response! The shepherds come, dirty and ritually unclean, into the very presence of the One who has come to make men clean. Though shepherds are not considered trustworthy witnesses in a court of law in Israel, they are entrusted with the message of the Messiah's arrival. As Mary and Joseph watch in wonder, they ponder the marvelous things that transpire. They contemplate the mercy of God and the outpouring of honor and worship offered by the Magi.

My prayer:

> *Dear Lord, please help these children to recognize Jesus as their treasure and to worship Him as the Son of God made flesh for their salvation. Please give them eyes that see and hearts that ponder the wonders of Your work in their own lives. And please increase their delight as they share the Messiah with others.*

Fourth Joyful Mystery
Presentation in the Temple
(Lk. 2:22-40)

Mary and Joseph are careful to obey the Law, including the laws concerning purification and coming to the Temple to make sacrifices. Like any ordinary mom, Mary carries her first-born to a particular door at the Temple. Busy priests may have had them wait in line; other couples are there, too, thinking their baby is just as good as Mary and Joseph's. Mary and Joseph, in humility, do not reveal they are the mother and foster father of the long-awaited Savior. When it is Jesus' turn, Mary hands Him to a priest who accepts Him and presents Him to the Lord.

A one-year-old lamb is offered—or a pair of turtledoves, if the couple is poor—as a holocaust to honor God as the Lord of life and to consecrate the first-born son. Mary and Joseph offer their sacrifice of two turtledoves for Jesus who *is* the Lord of life. Their sacrifice is offered in the Temple for the One who is Lord of the Temple. The typical prayer of a mother during this sacrifice was, "This child is more your child than mine." How true this was from Mary's lips!

Simeon, a "righteous and devout" man, inspired by the Holy Spirit, blesses Jesus, Mary, and Joseph. He praises God for letting him see the Promised One through whom will come salvation to the Gentiles as well as to all of Israel. Then he makes the following prophecy:

> Behold, this child is set for the fall and rising of many in Israel, and for a sign that is spoken against (and a sword will pierce through your own soul also), that thoughts out of many hearts may be revealed.

Mary and Joseph marvel at God's work in their lives through Jesus. As they follow God's will, they will have suffering as well as joy—Simeon's words confirm that. Mary had to face the future, most likely without Joseph's help (since the prophecy was about her specifically), with godly courage.

My prayer:

Dear Lord, please guide these children to be obedient in the small things as well as the big, just as Mary and Joseph were careful to obey all of the laws. Please strengthen them so that they can face an uncertain future, knowing the only One who knows the future. Just as Mary and Joseph left the Temple assured of Your grace to see them through whatever difficulties lay ahead, so let these children place their trust in You.

Fifth Joyful Mystery
Finding of Jesus in the Temple
(Lk. 2:41-52)

Mary and Joseph travel the three-day journey with twelve-year-old Jesus to participate in the yearly Passover in Jerusalem. This was Jesus' transition from boyhood to manhood. Mary and Joseph give Jesus the freedom to travel with others, or so they think, for the first full day after the Passover. However, when they cannot find Jesus among relatives and friends, they return a day's journey to Jerusalem diligently searching for Him, their concern growing greater by the hour. They have lost their only beloved Son.

For three days, Mary and Joseph cannot find Jesus until they go into the Temple. What joy and relief they feel, mixed with the normal frustration of parents who have lost a child for three days. Jesus, apparently unconcerned about His parents' whereabouts, is at home in the Temple, talking with the elders and amazing them with His insightful questions.

When Mary and Joseph question Jesus as to why He has done this, He questions them: "Did you not know that I must be in my Father's house?" He knows who He is to them as their child, but He also knows who He is to His Heavenly Father. Where else would *the* sacrificial Passover Lamb be but the Temple? Where else would *the* High Priest be but the Temple? In his eighth-century commentary on the Gospel of Luke, Venerable Bede writes:

He does not upbraid them—Mary and Joseph—for searching for their son, but He raises the eyes of their souls to appreciate what He owes Him whose Eternal Son He is.

Mary and Joseph have ordinary knowledge. They do not comprehend fully—but they do tuck away these thoughts, pondering them in their hearts. Jesus leaves with them, assuming His subordinate role as their obedient child. As Luke records, "Jesus increased in wisdom and in stature, and in favor with God and man."

My prayer:

Dear Lord, please help these children prioritize prayer with a deepening sense of the One to whom they belong, just as Jesus did in the Temple. If sudden misfortune comes, let them follow Mary and Joseph's example, bearing the difficulties in union with Jesus, trusting themselves to Your will, pondering Your work in their lives, and searching for Your presence in the tabernacle. Like Jesus, let them grow in wisdom and in stature, and in favor with both God and man.

First Sorrowful Mystery
The Agony in the Garden
(Mt. 26:36-56; Mk. 14:32-50; Lk. 22:39-53; Jn.18:1-11)

Following the Last Supper, Jesus and His disciples (minus Judas who is betraying Him) leave Jerusalem, cross the Kidron Valley, and enter the Garden of Gethsemane. This is the same path King David traveled with his followers when his son Absalom betrayed him.

Jesus draws His three closest disciples—Peter, James, and John—to be nearest Him. The ones who have seen His glory on the Mount of Transfiguration are about to witness His agony. He wants the consolation of their presence and prayers, and yet He needs to be alone. After Jesus urges the disciples to be watchful and prayerful, He goes a short distance from them where He pours out His heart to His Heavenly Father.

Jesus' horrific ordeal is about to begin and He knows it. He asks His Heavenly Father to let the suffering pass. Three times He falls on His face, praying fervently in agony, sweating great drops of blood. Each time He yields His will to His Heavenly Father's will—He wills to do God's will, no matter the cost.

After each time, Jesus returns to His disciples only to find them sleeping from crippling fear and perplexity. They are unable to give Him the consolation He needs.

Mary is absent. Her absence is a part of her suffering as well as Jesus'. Somewhere she is praying for Him, but she is unable to be with Him.

Before He returns to the disciples for the last time, an angel comes to strengthen Him. It is the last time angelic succor is evident until the Resurrection. Even heaven's consolation is withdrawn; this is part of the suffering Jesus must endure in redeeming us.

My prayer:

Dearest Lord, You faced incredible suffering and still yielded Your will to Your Heavenly Father's. Please help these children to pour their hearts out to You whenever they are in anguish and, at the same time, actively place their trust in You and Your divine will. Please help us to support them by being watchful and prayerful, unlike Your disciples in the Garden.

Second Sorrowful Mystery
Scourging at the Pillar
(Mt. 27:24-26; Mk. 15:1-15; Lk. 22:63-65; 23:13-25; Jn. 18:28-19:1)

After the betrayal of Judas' kiss, Jesus is arrested. His disciples, filled with fear, abandon Him. Later in the evening, Peter three times denies even knowing Him.

Jesus is taken through a series of trials before secular and religious officials. No one knows quite what to do with Him. The religious leaders pressure the political leaders because they want Him dead. The political leaders fear the reaction of the people if they free Him. Finally, Pilate makes the decision for crucifixion and sends Jesus to be scourged by the Roman guards, just as Jesus had prophesied.

Not only is Jesus rejected by His own people, but He suffers at the hands of Gentiles who hate His race. These guards strip Him, adding the humiliation of nakedness, and make Him bend over a pillar so that He will feel the full brunt of each blow.

Then they take turns whipping Him with cat-o'-nine-tails—strips of leather with embedded rocks and pieces of metal. Jesus receives thirty-nine lashes, one less than what was believed would kill a man. They ready Him for crucifixion at the same time the Passover lambs were being prepared for slaughter in the Temple. And like the lambs led to slaughter, He remains silent, which only further aggravates those who inflict pain on Him (Is. 53:7).

Mary remembers that Jesus predicted His own suffering and death. She is in the crowd when Pilate sentences Him to scourging and crucifixion. Though she cannot be near Him, her sorrowful heart prays for Him as He endures these stripes for our salvation (Is. 53:5).

My prayer:

> *Dear Lord, You were scourged for these children's sins of passion. Please produce the fruit of the Spirit of self-control in their lives. If others misuse or hurt them, please strengthen them, by Jesus' example, to overcome evil with good.*

Third Sorrowful Mystery
The Crowning with Thorns
(Mt. 27:11-27)

Throughout His ministry, Jesus proclaims that the kingdom of God has come. When Pilate questions Him, He says that His kingdom is not of this world. Though the Jews accuse Jesus of insurrection, based on His claim of kingship, they object to Pilate's inscription on the Cross, "Jesus of Nazareth, King of the Jews."

In mockery, after they whip Him, the Roman guards "dress up" Jesus as a king. They place a beautiful garment of purple on His bleeding shoulders, press a crown made of thorns on His head, and hand Him a reed for a scepter. Then they bow before Him as if He were a king. They blindfold Him and hit Him, taunting Him to identify who is hitting or spitting on Him.

In ancient times, as a sign of conquering the land, soldiers crowned their victorious leader with a crown made from twigs from the captured area. Though the Roman soldiers did not intend to honor Jesus, the crown of thorns they made was, in a sense, a victor's wreath—Jesus *was* conquering the whole earth which had been cursed with thorns since the fall of man in the Garden of Eden (Gen. 3:17-18). Though the soldiers thought they were in control, Jesus was, in fact, laying down His life in order to redeem the world through the very sufferings He had predicted they would inflict.

Though Mary may not know exactly what is happening to Him at the time, she can imagine what He is suffering. She can only wait and see if she can, in any way, accompany Him to the Cross.

My prayer:

Dear Lord, You said that the world that hated You would also reject your followers. Please prepare these children for whatever suffering they may have to endure as they follow You. Please grant them the grace of perseverance in the face of tribulation. Help them know that they will reign with You provided they suffer with You.

Fourth Sorrowful Mystery
Carrying the Cross
(Lk. 23:26-32)

Jesus has endured much torturous suffering. Now begins the final arduous part of His journey to Calvary. He carries His own Cross a third of a mile, winding barefoot through the stony streets of His beloved Jerusalem. He follows a route that takes Him out of the city gates because no criminal is put to death inside the city. As He staggers and falls under His burden, the people jeer at Him and mock Him, gloating over His misery.

On this brief but very difficult journey, Jesus encounters different people. Simon the Cyrene, minding his own business, is pressed into service to carry Jesus' Cross the remainder of the way to Golgotha. The guards were not kind to Jesus; they wanted to be sure He did not die before being crucified. Next, Jesus speaks to some women of Jerusalem who are weeping for Him. He urges them to focus their concern on the judgment coming to them and to their children in Jerusalem—judgment for all of the innocent blood that has been shed, including His own.

Jesus also encounters His Blessed Mother. They are one in spirit, one in heart. Now Mary can see the consequence of all of the suffering her beloved Son has already endured, and her heart feels as if it is being pierced by a sword, just as Simeon had foretold. They cannot speak, but their eyes connect: His look says, "This is the will of God," and hers says, "Behold the handmaid of the Lord." Each embraces the suffering of the other, knowing that the world's redemption will be the fruit of their sacrificial gift. Mary does not interfere with His self-offering, but she accompanies Him to Calvary, remains at His feet, and offers her suffering in union with His.

My prayer:

Dear Lord, please help these children to understand what You have endured for their salvation. Thank You that Mary didn't thwart Your self-offering to alleviate her own suffering, but rather accompanied You to the Cross. May these children draw close to Your Sacred Heart and to Your mother's Immaculate Heart as they walk the way of the Cross with You and Your mother.

Fifth Sorrowful Mystery
The Crucifixion of Our Lord
(Mt. 27:33-61; Mk. 15:22-47; Lk. 23:33-56; Jn. 19:18-42)

The soldiers want to be finished with this execution. They place Jesus roughly on the Cross and hammer nails through His wrists and ankles. Then the Cross is lifted and dropped into a hole, jarring His bones and straining His muscles. In addition to

His hunger, thirst, exhaustion, and blood loss, Jesus begins a slow and painful death by asphyxiation. The mocking continues from religious leaders at the foot of the Cross as well as from passersby, yet Jesus does not respond in anger or bitterness.

With slow, pain-filled utterances He asks the Father to forgive those who are killing Him rather than cursing them as other crucified victims would be tempted to do. He extends mercy to the repentant thief, which offers hope to many for the possibility of a death-bed conversion, and He provides for the needs of His mother and the Church by giving His mother and His beloved disciple to each another—an example to all of us who claim to be beloved disciples to take Mary into our homes as well.

In addition to all of His other sufferings, He quotes Psalm 22, "My God, my God, why hast thou forsaken me?" As His consummate act of total self-donation, out of His love for the Father and for us, He takes upon Himself every suffering, including a sense of abandonment by the Father. He lays down His life by choice—it is not taken from Him (Jn. 10:17-18).

Jesus maintains alertness to the end, expressing His thirst "in order to fulfill the Scriptures"—He drinks the fruit of the vine as He enters His kingdom through His death. Then Jesus declares, "It is finished"—He has drunk the dregs of the cup of suffering for our salvation.

Then Mary hears Jesus quote a familiar verse from the Psalms, an evening prayer mothers taught their children, "Father, into thy hands I commit my spirit!" (Lk. 23:46; cf. Ps. 31:5). As He breathes His last, the calm is shattered—darkness descends, though it is only three in the afternoon; the earth shakes, rocks are split open, and the three-foot-thick curtain separating the Holy of Holies from the Holy Place in the Temple is torn from top to bottom.

Mary stays to the end. She watches Him relinquish His Spirit and suffers the loss of His life as only a mother can, all the while knowing what His sacrifice means for the salvation of the world. She sees the soldiers pierce His side—one more indignity added to all of the others—and water and blood flow, evidencing His death. When the soldiers take His body from the Cross, Mary cradles the body of her beloved Son. Then she gives His body to Joseph of Arimathea to be placed in His new tomb.

My prayer:

Dear Lord, please help the children to understand the sacrificial love You have for them—a love so great that You sent Your beloved Son to the Cross as a holocaust for them. Please help them make sense of their own sufferings in light of Jesus' sufferings. And please help them to deny themselves and take up their own cross daily as they follow You.

First Glorious Mystery
The Resurrection of Our Lord
(Mt. 27:62-28:15; Mk. 16:1-14;
Lk. 23:54-24:43; Jn. 20:1-29; 1 Cor. 15)

Imagine the scene: It's a full moon—it always is at Passover. A large stone covers the cave-tomb's entrance, sealed with the high priest's seal. Soldiers stand watch because Jesus' enemies had heard His words about resurrection and they are afraid that His disciples would steal His body. Jesus' enemies rest more easily now; the soldiers are watchful of sounds and movement around the tomb, never thinking something is happening *inside* the grave!

By the power of the Holy Spirit, Jesus rises from the dead, taking back the life He so willingly laid down for our salvation. Why was His mother not at the tomb? She alone believed the words He had prophesied concerning His death *and* resurrection. She knew His body would not be there.

Early in the morning of the third day after His death, the women who watched Jesus die (except for His mother) return to prepare His body properly for burial. The massive stone blocking the tomb has been rolled away. The soldiers have left to report the body's disappearance. The women are frightened and incredulous when an angel announces the news of Jesus' Resurrection. Is it possible? Then Jesus reveals Himself to them.

Immediately, the women go to the apostles to tell them the wonderful news. The apostles do not believe them; however, John and Peter race to the tomb. John stops at the door and peers in; Peter dashes inside. Once they look inside the empty tomb, John believes Jesus is raised from the dead; Peter is amazed but unsure. The linen bands are still there as if Jesus' body simply passed through them like light.

Jesus appears to two disciples on the road to Emmaus and reveals Himself in the breaking of bread with them. Then Jesus makes a number of appearances to the disciples and other followers over the course of forty days. Jesus' Resurrection changes the cowardly disciples, who were hiding from the authorities, into bold witnesses for Christ.

My prayer:

Dear Lord, may the same power of the Holy Spirit that raised Jesus from the dead empower these children to be bold witnesses to Your life, death, and Resurrection. Please strengthen their faith in the resurrected Lord so that they know they have not believed in vain.

Second Glorious Mystery
The Ascension of Our Lord
(Mt. 28:16-20; Mk. 16:15-19;
Lk. 24:44-53; Jn. 21:1-23; Acts 1:3-12)

For forty days, Jesus prepares His disciples for His departure. He appears to them on numerous occasions, opens the Scriptures to them, and tells them about the ministry of the Holy Spirit who will be sent to them as His gift from heaven. He meets Peter at a charcoal fire—reminiscent of another charcoal fire at which Peter denied the Lord three times—and asks Him three times if he loves Him. Each time Jesus responds to Peter's affirmation with a call to feed the people of the Lord.

Jesus leads Mary and the disciples up the Mount of Olives. From there, they can see the Temple, the hill of Golgotha where He laid down His life, Bethlehem in the distance, and beyond that, the Judean wilderness where He had been tested following His Baptism.

At the top of the Mount, Jesus raises His hand in blessing and tells Mary and the disciples to wait in Jerusalem until they receive the Holy Spirit. Then He commissions them:

> Go therefore and make disciples of all nations, baptizing them in the name of the Father and of the Son and of the Holy Spirit, teaching them to observe all that I have commanded you (Mt. 28:19-20).

While Jesus blesses them, He ascends, body and soul, by His own power, to heaven. As they stare after Him, He disappears into the *shekinah* or "glory" cloud of God to take up His rightful place on a throne at the right hand of the Father. Jesus, the perfect high priest, returns to His Father with His glorified humanity into the heavenly Holy of Holies to be the once-and-for-all-time perpetual offering to the Father (cf. Heb. 10:12-14).

Then angels appear to Mary and the disciples. The angels assure them that Jesus is now in heaven. They are to return to Jerusalem, as Jesus commanded, to await the gift of the Holy Spirit. No longer are they full of dread at His departure; their hearts are full of joy and anticipation at what will happen next.

What about Mary? This is the fulfillment of her walk with Our Lord on earth. Jesus' Ascension is the culmination of the Annunciation, for Jesus has returned to the Father from whence He came. She received Him; now she releases Him back to the Father. She shares in the great joy and anticipation of wonderful things yet to come, and returns with the disciples to await the coming of the Holy Spirit in Jerusalem.

My prayer:

> *Dear Lord, please help the children to see Jesus both as their high priest and as the perpetual offering in the heavenly Holy of Holies for their sins. Help them to receive Him as such in the Eucharist. Thank You for the reminder that heaven, not earth, is our home. Please help them to practice detachment today, so that they may be heavenly minded enough to do earthly good.*

Third Glorious Mystery
Descent of the Holy Spirit
(Acts 1:12-2:27)

Just before Jesus ascends to the Father, He tells Mary and the disciples to return to Jerusalem to await the gift of the Holy Spirit. The Holy Spirit will empower them to be His witnesses "in Jerusalem and in all Judea and Samaria and to the end of the earth" (Acts 1:8). They do as He says. They return to the same upper room where they had celebrated the Last Supper with Him. And for nine days they pray the first novena in anticipation of the coming of the Holy Spirit.

On the ninth day, the Holy Spirit comes and fills Mary and the disciples gathered in the upper room. They speak in tongues, including the languages of many visitors in Jerusalem from other countries who have gathered to celebrate Pentecost, the Feast of First Fruits. The disciples declare the mighty deeds of God to all who would listen.

Then Peter addresses the crowd, witnessing to Jesus' life, death, and Resurrection. About 3,000 people state their desire for repentance, Baptism, and reception of the Holy Spirit. They are the "first fruits" of a new kind of harvest—a harvest of souls at the birth of the Church.

My prayer:

Dear Lord, please pour out Your Spirit on these children, and give them courage to share the Gospel with others and see them come to faith. Thank You for giving birth to the Church at Pentecost and using Your chosen instrument, Peter, to bring 3,000 converts to the Church that day. Please help our children grow in their appreciation for Your Church and Your chosen instrument, Our Holy Father.

Fourth Glorious Mystery
The Bodily Assumption of the Blessed Virgin Mary
(Rev. 11:19–12:17)

John testifies in the Book of Revelation, "Then God's temple in heaven was opened, and the ark of his covenant was seen within his temple" (Rev. 11:19). Any Jew reading this would have his heart skip a beat. The ark of the covenant? The sacred wooden box which contained the Ten Commandments, manna, Aaron's rod, and the throne of the mercy seat, missing for hundreds of years, found in heaven?

John continues, "[A] great portent appeared in heaven, a woman clothed with the sun, with the moon under her feet, and on her head a crown of twelve stars" (Rev. 12:1). John sees a woman's body in glory and splendor—the new ark of the covenant which held the living Word of God and the living bread come down from heaven, Jesus. In other words, he sees Mary.

John goes on to describe that the woman, whom others are seeking to destroy, is with child. His portrayal leaves no doubt—the woman in the passage is Mary. Why is this significant? John describes Mary's body in heaven as well as her soul. How can that be?

Mary was saved from the moment of conception by her Son, Jesus. Mary acknowledges this great work of God through her Savior in the Magnificat—by grace, she is saved from the effects of sin and preserved from actual sin. Corruption of the flesh is a consequence of sin; if Mary did not experience sin, her body would not need to undergo corruption.

Mary was assumed into heaven, body and soul, by the power of the Holy Spirit. Unlike Jesus, who ascended to the Father by His own power, Mary was assumed bodily by God's power. Her bodily Assumption demonstrates the transforming power of the Spirit in eventually granting each of us resurrected bodies. She is, in a sense, a foreshadowing of things to come for all believers.

My prayer:

Dear Lord, thank You for taking Mary, body and soul, into heaven, completing Your great work of grace in her heart and life. Please fill these children with hope of their own resurrection exemplified in Mary's bodily Assumption. And please help them draw closer to her so that she can draw their hearts closer to You.

Fifth Glorious Mystery
The Coronation of Mary as Queen of Heaven
(1 Kings 2:10-25; Rev. 12:1)

When Solomon, the son of David, was king, he welcomed his mother, Bathsheba, into his court. He paid her homage, bowed before her, and requested that she sit at his right hand while he ruled (1 Kings 2:10-25). His practice established a new role for the *gebirah* or queen mother of the king. She had special access to him, because of close relationship, and she made special requests on behalf of others. She was queen mother by virtue of her son, the king.

Jesus, the Son of David, ascends to His throne of heaven. When Mary is assumed into heaven, He welcomes her as the *gebirah*, or queen mother, of heaven. She is queen mother *because* her Son is King of Kings and Lord and Lords. Just as the earthly *gebirah* was seated on a throne, so Mary is given a throne. That's why John sees her as having a crown on her head. She has special access to Jesus, due to their close relationship as mother and Son, and she makes requests on behalf of others.

Not only is she Jesus' mother, but she is the spiritual mother of "those who keep the commandments of God and bear testimony to [him]" (Rev. 12:17). Since we want to keep God's commandments and bear testimony to the Lord, we are, in fact, her children. The requests Mary makes of Jesus are those of a mother on behalf of us, her children. Since Jesus is the one mediator between God and man, it is through Jesus that Mary mediates grace. She draws our hearts closer each day to her Son, telling us, "Do whatever he tells you" (Jn. 2:5).

My prayer:

Dear Lord, thank You for the gift of Your mother as our spiritual mother. Please help these children to draw closer to Your mother's heart and to ask her for prayer as queen mother of heaven. Through her intercession, may they faithfully love, honor, and obey You.

Penny for Your Thoughts

I cannot remember a time I did not believe in God. All of my life, my parents have directed my thoughts toward Him in worship, thanksgiving, and supplication. I will always be grateful for the gift of knowing God through my parents' mediation. What I did not know, however, was that my spiritual mother, Mary, was also a part of my life from early on. When I became a child of the Father through the Son, the mother of the Son became my mother as well.

As I talk with friends who have been raised Catholic, I find they speak as naturally of Mary as their mother as I speak of my Heavenly Father as my Father. It's an adjustment to discover as an adult that I have had a special mother without knowing it. I try to include her in my daily life, asking her to pray for me, thanking her for her motherly care for me long before I knew she was there, and developing my understanding of her role.

A college student shared a creative idea with me: Whenever her mom found a penny, she would give it to her and say, "Remember, your mother loves you." The student testified that even as an adult, whenever she finds a penny, her mother's words of love echo in her ears.

I have adapted this idea and made it a kind of sacramental. Whenever I find a penny, I thank God for my mother's love for me and for Mary's motherly love for me. Then I give it to one of my children with this reminder, "Remember. Mommy loves you and Mary, your spiritual mother, loves you." My own experience with motherhood deepens my love for Mary as my mother—it is a joy to imagine her love for me and her desire to assist me as I love and care for my own children.

To God Be the Glory

We carefully differentiate between veneration of Mary, which is good and right, and adoration of Mary, which the Catholic Church condemns as idolatry. For Protestants, worship consists of songs, prayer, and a sermon. On a Marian feast day, since Catholics have songs about Mary, prayers to Mary, and a homily about Mary, Protestants can feel offended that we have "worshipped" her. However, as Catholics, we define adoration as sacrifice and veneration as honoring those whom God honors. For example, we would never offer Mary's body as a sacrifice nor do we sacrifice to her, though we do honor Mary and the saints as, we believe, God does.

Marian feast days are great opportunities to increase our family's appreciation for God's work through Mary. Candlelight and special desserts highlight the specialness of the day—there's nothing quite like fire and sugar to get kids' attention.

I find it helpful to draw my children's hearts toward Mary by describing her part in the mysteries of the Rosary or her place at the various Stations of the Cross. On a recent pilgrimage to the Holy Land, we talked about her role in salvation history as we visited Nazareth, Cana, Bethlehem, and Jerusalem. As our appreciation grows for Mary, our gratitude grows for God who gave her to us.

One day Scott called to our infant son, Jeremiah, "Come to Daddy!" We both watched as he made a gallant effort to crawl as quickly as he could on the slick wood floor. Seeing Jeremiah's struggle, I ran to his side, scooped him up, and raced over to Scott, dropping him into Scott's waiting arms. As we laughed together, Scott and I suddenly looked at each other and said, "Mary." I had never before understood why Catholic friends would say that Mary was a quicker way to get to the Father through the Son; now I had just enacted physically what she does spiritually. She helps us in our struggle to reach the Father.

Just as an artist is honored by the appreciation others give his greatest work of art, so the Father is glorified by our acknowledgement of His work in Mary—Mary *is* His masterpiece. Her mission is not to get us to look at her, but to look with her to her Son and His Father. We do not detract from God's glory when we honor Mary as our mother—we demonstrate His glory. In imitation of Jesus, we love and honor His Father as our Father. In imitation of Jesus, we love and honor His mother as our mother.

As beloved disciples at the foot of the Cross, let's welcome Our Lord's mother as our own into our hearts and homes. Let's imitate Mary's faith-filled obedience with our own "Yes" to the call of God on our lives. And let's invoke Mary's assistance to guide us to her Son, and through Him to the Father, by the working of the Holy Spirit.

Kimberly Hahn is an internationally known speaker and author. Along with her husband Scott, she is coauthor of Rome Sweet Home *(Ignatius Press, 1994), which chronicles their celebrated conversion to the Catholic faith.*

Chapter X

Mary and the Church

Sean Innerst

"I would lead you and bring you into the house of my mother,
and into the chamber of her that conceived me" (Song 8:2).

It might seem that "Mary and the Church" would be a redundancy in a book dedicated to the mystery of the Mother of God in Scripture. Isn't it the case that all the chapters in this book converge to portray the connection between Mary and the Church? Well, yes, one would hope so. But without repeating what is found in all the pieces of the mosaic that the chapters of this volume represent, it is certainly useful to step back and get a glimpse of the whole picture of who Mary is.

To some extent, that "whole picture" of Mary is suggested by the quote at the head of this chapter from the Song of Solomon, also known as the Song of Songs. That poetic dialogue of love between a groom and his future bride has often been interpreted, by Jews and Christians, as a mystical colloquy between the soul and her God. From antiquity, the Church has borrowed verses from the Song of Solomon for the liturgies of her Marian feasts, but the oldest patristic texts also liken the lover in the poem to

Christ and the beloved to the Church. This fact alone points to the ancient faith of the Church, that there is a mysterious, mystical identity between Mary and the Church. That is the import of those famous words from the Second Vatican Council that, "in the most Blessed Virgin the Church has already reached that perfection whereby she exists without spot or wrinkle" (LG 65).

That the Bride or Beloved in the Song of Solomon can be interpreted as representing on different levels Mary, the Church, or the individual soul is shown by the fact that the words quoted above are not, as one might first guess, spoken by the lover or the groom, but by the bride. She longs to take her future spouse to the house of her mother so that she can be like a sister to him and, thereby, show him more affection. (In Jewish society of the time brothers and sisters were allowed greater latitude for public signs of affection, like hand holding and embracing, than those who were courting.) When interpreted in this way, the text in question could be seen as an invitation from the Church, as Bride, for a greater intimacy with her mother Mary. The home of the bride of Christ is the house of Mary.

For the purposes of this chapter, then, I would like to suggest in these words of the bride from the Songs of Solomon an invitation to our brother (and sister) Protestants to enter the house of the mother, our common mother, so that we, too, might exchange the embrace that siblings in faith should share. I'd like to do so by drawing out further this mystical identity between Mary and the Church.

Scriptural Mother

That there is a kind of identity between Mary and the Church may at first seem to be saying too much, but it is really the best refutation of the most fundamental misunderstanding of the Church's Marian devotion: that we worship Mary as divine. To say that there is a mystical identity between Mary and the Church is to say that the Church, called together by God to worship Him alone, is Marian in her worship of God, which is the very opposite of mariolatry. We do not offer Mary the worship that is owed to God, but rather the Church strives to be Marian in offering God the worship we owe to Him.

There are countless scriptural passages that support the mystical identity between Mary and the Church. This assertion would likely surprise our Protestant brothers and sisters. "Mary has so few words and makes so few appearances in the New Testament. The little we ought to say about Mary is confirmed by the very dearth of references we find to her," they might say.

But that is not the way the first Christians read the Scriptures. With the typological precedent set by Saints Peter and Paul,[1] and indeed by Jesus Himself[2]—along with an intuition born of faith—the Fathers and doctors of the Church saw Mary represented everywhere: in the holy women of ancient Israel, Hannah, Deborah, Ruth, Judith, and Esther, and as the antithesis to Eve, untying the knot of her disobedience and becoming a new Eve (cf. Catechism, nos. 489, 494). These heroines, whose greatness is often linked to a gratuitous gift of God which lifts them from a humble position to one of influence, together comprise the mat-

---

[1] A "typological" reading of the Old Testament by the New Testament writers can be seen in passages like Romans 5:14, in which Adam is called a "type" of Christ, that is, a figurative, prophetic foreshadowing of Christ as the new or second Adam. In 1 Peter 3:20-21, the apostle asserts the same sort of typological relationship between the flood in the time of Noah and Christian Baptism. In 1 Corinthians 10, Saint Paul uses a typological reading of the Exodus events at the Red Sea and the bestowal of manna and water from the rock to explicate the responsibilities incumbent upon Christians after the reception of Baptism and the Eucharist. This perception of faith—that God's plan of salvation has a unity that enables us to see prophetic foreshadowings of present Christian realities in the persons and events of the Old Testament—has prompted the Church to see Mary present in type or figure in the Old Testament (cf. Catechism, nos. 128-29).

[2] In Matthew 12, Jesus compares Himself to the Temple (v. 6), Jonah (v. 41), and Solomon (v. 42), in each case asserting that He is "greater" than these. Likewise, in John 6:31-35, Jesus draws a comparison between the manna in the wilderness and Himself as "the bread of life." Although in all such comparisons Jesus is advantaged, always "greater than" that to which He is compared, it is clear that the comparison also enriches the theological content of the realities to which He compares Himself. In this way, He reveals new meaning in the realities of the Old Testament and salvation history generally, which the Church continues to explore by a spiritual or typological reading of these realities.

ter for an Old Testament theology of woman that finds perhaps its fullest expression in "daughter Zion," a feminine personification of Israel.[3] The ancients also saw Mary's virginal integrity symbolized by the virgin earth from which Adam was made, the unconsumed burning bush, the closed door of the Temple, the sealed fountain, and many other figures. The whole of the Old Testament was seen as pregnant, so to speak, with these Marian images that only came to light when the fullness of time had come in Christ.[4]

As a matter of fact, in Galatians 4:4, arguably the oldest scriptural reference to Mary, Saint Paul specifically states the "fullness of time" occurred when the eternal Son was "born of woman." He goes on to say that we have now gained adoption as sons of the same Father. The ancient Christians were quick to draw the obvious conclusion about the identity of the mother of these new sons in the Son, who was Himself "born of woman." No doubt this would be the same "woman" at the wedding in Cana of Galilee in John 2, and the "woman" who received the beloved disciple as an adopted son at the foot of the Cross of her first-born Son in John 19. Jesus was Mary's "first-born son" (Lk. 2:7), as well as God the Father's, and so obviously in both cases "the first-born among many brethren" (Rom. 8:29).

---

[3] Joseph Ratzinger, *Daughter Zion* (San Francisco: Ignatius Press, 1983), 9-29.
[4] *Ibid.*, 12 *et seq.* Cardinal Joseph Ratzinger, drawing on the insights of Louis Bouyer's *Woman in the Church*, shows that "the figure of woman occupies an irreplaceable place in the overall texture of Old Testament faith and piety" (13). This feminine principle, which is the proper spousal complement to the divine Groom in the prophetic literature of the Old Testament, finds her "personal epitome" in Mary. Cardinal Ratzinger notes that "the New Testament refers back to the mothers of the Old Testament, to the theology of daughter Zion, and probably also to Eve, and then ties the three lines of development together" (25). Cardinal Ratzinger also shows that the virginal and bridal character of Israel and Mary stands in marked contrast to the cult prostitution of the surrounding cultures, making marriage a precisely theological representation of fidelity, and fornication or adultery the contrary representation of idolatry. See also Sean Innerst, "The Marital Plan of God," *Lay Witness* (June 1996), 4-5, 26.

Saint Paul writes:

> When we cry "Abba! Father!" it is the Spirit himself bearing witness
> with our spirit that we are children of God, and if children, then
> heirs, heirs of God and fellow heirs with Christ (Rom. 8:15-17).

If we are heirs with Christ, then should that not include the
mother He bequeathed to John as His last will and testament?
And so it is that the same Spirit who taught the Church to cry out
"Abba," taught her to cry out "Mama" to Mary.

When the "woman" of John's Gospel later appears to us in
Revelation 12:1-6 and 17 "clothed with the sun" and bearing not
just one son "who is to rule all the nations with a rod of iron,"
but "the rest of her offspring" who "keep the commandments of
God" and "bear testimony to Jesus," the faithful recognize Mary.
Just as her appearance precipitates conflict in the heavens in
John's vision of the Apocalypse (cf. Rev. 12:7), she seems always
to be a point of conflict in the Church, a stumbling block like the
Son to whom she gave flesh.

There are no great innovations here, no great leaps into the
theological stratosphere. These are just fitting conclusions, drawn
from both the Old and New Testaments, about who Mary was
and still is to us.[5]

"Well," you might say, "I see now that Mary could be a
spiritual mother to Christians, but how does that demonstrate
an identity between the Church and Mary?" A first and perhaps
unlikely answer can be found in the common Protestant reading

---

[5] *Ibid.*, 32. Ratzinger shows that the Marian dogmas which seem at first not to be contained
in individual passages of the New Testament "become visible only to a mode of perception that accepts this unity [of the Old and New Testaments], i.e., within a perspective
which makes its own the 'typological' interpretation." He goes on to remark, "Wherever
the unity of Old and New Testaments disintegrates, the place of a healthy Mariology is
lost." Once our separated Christian brethren begin to read Scripture in this unified way
so common to the Christians of earlier centuries they can no longer say, "The Bible says
little about Mary and so should we." Read in this way, the whole Bible is patently Marian.

of Revelation 12. Most Protestants will say that the woman of that passage represents Israel. They are not wrong, but only half right. Mary, as was said above, is the scriptural fulfillment of many of the women of Israel. She is more than that, even the very embodiment of virgin "daughter Zion."[6]

If the "woman" of Revelation 12 can adequately represent the whole of Israel bringing forth Christ and the Church, then why couldn't that "woman" on another level—and without negating or even obscuring that other symbolism—be Mary, the woman to whom John often applies the title "woman," and *the* woman who actually did give birth to Christ? Once we admit the principle that Scripture can use persons, places, or things as symbols in an evocative or figurative way, there is no reason to arbitrarily limit that principle only to those evocations that fit one's particular theology or ecclesiology, as long as they are in accord with the rest of Scripture.[7] If *a* "woman" can represent Israel, why then can't Mary, *the* "woman" at the marriage feast of Cana and the foot of the Cross, represent the new Israel of God, the Church?

Marian Presence

One of the qualities of a mystery is that it is multiform. Christ, *the* mystery of God's self-communication is at once Son of God, Son of Man, and Son of Mary. He is the Head of the Body, the Church, and yet we say that the Church is the Body of Christ. This multiformity, by which deep mysteries never seem to find full or even adequate expression in any one sign or symbol, is evident throughout the Scriptures. These revealed images or

---

[6] *Ibid.*, 24. Zion is the hill in Jerusalem on which the Temple was built and so symbolizes in the Old Testament the religious aspirations of the people of Israel. The use of the phrase "daughter of Zion" in Jeremiah 4:31 and Micah 4:10, in which she is shown bringing forth a child, may be echoed in Revelation 12.

[7] A Catholic mode of interpretation would also require that these typological evocations be in accord with those drawn out of the text by the saints, Fathers, and doctors of the Church who have gone before us.

symbols that are used to express divine mysteries move us in the direction of real understanding, but they always fall short because the mysteries themselves are always more than can be expressed.

Mary's part in the "plan of the mystery" (Eph. 3:9) is no less multiform, no less complex. The Church has always recognized that Mary is at once daughter of the Father, spouse of the Spirit, and mother of the Son. She is simultaneously virgin and mother. She is entirely consecrated to the Lord and yet wholly given over to the service of the little family of Nazareth. None of these roles is exclusive of the others, of course. They are not so because, as you may have noticed, they are expressions of familial relationships. Just as Jesus is Son of God and Mary, Mary is daughter, mother, and spouse in relation to the Persons of the Trinity all at once and without detriment to the other relations. And those relations with the triune God only encourage and enhance her relationship with Joseph and, in fact, with all of her spiritual children in the Church.

But here we must stress that the identity between Mary and the Church is a mysterious identity, more than merely symbolic or metaphorical and yet less than an absolute, metaphysical identity. To put it best we should say, not that the Church *is* Mary, but that the Church is Marian. There is a presence of Mary wherever the Church is.[8] What we are describing is one aspect of the mystery of communion expressed in Hebrews 12:22-23:

> But you have come to Mount Zion and to the city of the living God, the heavenly Jerusalem, and to innumerable angels in festal gathering, and to the assembly of the first-born who are enrolled in heaven, and to a judge who is God of all, and to the spirits of just men made perfect.

---

[8] See James T. O'Connor's reflections on the quality of this presence of Mary with particular reference to the Real Presence of Christ in the Blessed Sacrament in *The Hidden Manna* (San Francisco: Ignatius Press, 1988), 341-53.

Church's Children

In Baptism each believer is enfolded in a whole network of relationships, beginning with Christ Himself and including all the members of the Body of Christ, brothers and sisters living and dead, the whole host of heaven, and that woman who from the time of the Fathers of the Church has been identified with Zion in a particular way as "daughter Zion." All of these relationships have God the Father as their origin and goal, and await that glorious day when all things are subjected to Christ and by Christ to the Father, so that "God may be everything to every one" (1 Cor. 15:28).

Those relationships in Christ are multiform for us too. Christ is our brother, we are brothers and sisters to one another, and we are sons and daughters of the Father. None of those various relationships is harmed in any way by the others. Now, to those who might say that Mary ought not to be identified with the Church because the Church is the Body of Christ, we should ask, "Does our sonship in Christ supplant Christ as only Son of the Father?" No, of course not. It is *in* Christ's unique sonship that we are incorporated into our sonship. In the same way, Mary's mystical identity with the Church does not supplant the relation of the Body of Christ to its Head. Nor is our identity as members of the Body of Christ somehow effaced by our mystical incorporation into the Marian Church.

In fact, the first mystical union between a believer and Christ was between Mary and Jesus. She was the first member of the Body of Christ, but the manner of her union with Him surpasses that of any other. She was not only mystically united to Christ in His mystical body, but also physically united to Him by the act of giving Him a physical body. The Church is always giving new birth to Christ, in that new members of the Body of Christ are constantly being born by the sacramental activity of the Church. It's just that sort of insight that led so many of the Fathers and medieval theologians to use phrases in reference to the Church like "Christ's Mother," "Mother of Christ," or even "God's

Mother"![9] We are precisely made more fully the body of Christ by spiritually entering into the womb of the mother who bore Him. One of the ways in which we come to gain "the measure of the stature of the fulness of Christ . . . to grow up in every way into him who is the head" is to enter the Marian womb of the Church where "the whole body, joined and knit together . . . upbuilds itself in love" (Eph. 4:13, 15-16).

I don't think it is straining the text to see in Jesus' conversation with Nicodemus in John 3 a reflection of John's own experience of Marian sonship when he recalls for us the words, "How can a man be born when he is old? Can he enter a second time into his mother's womb and be born?" And the answer of the Son, who from the Cross gave John to His sorrowing mother and she to him, is no less suggestive of the Marian Church, "Truly, truly, I say to you, unless one is born from above, he cannot see the kingdom of God" (Jn. 3:3).

Christ Himself was "born from above" into the water of Mary's womb by the power of the Holy Spirit. Should not His follower undergo the same Marian birth at the font of Baptism, simultaneously becoming a son of God and a son of Mary, and thereby also a son of Mother Church? Is it any wonder, then, that the Church has always drawn a parallel between the water of the baptismal font and the watery womb of a mother? Seen from this perspective, the Marian identification with the Church is really no more than a direct extension of the identification of Christ with the Body of Christ, the Church. Just as His human

---

[9] Hugo Rahner, *Our Lady and the Church* (New York: Pantheon Books, 1961), 37-44, 69-79. Rahner's profound work is an extended treatment of this "Mariology of the Church" to which readers who are interested in learning more should refer. He shows that the "Church as the Mystical Mother of God" is present in the theology of the Church from the time of Hippolytus, citing other figures such as Origen, Augustine, Gregory the Great, the Venerable Bede, as well as lesser knowns, such as Methodius of Philippi, Anastasius of Sinai, and Haymo of Halberstadt. I owe thanks to Professor John Saward for introducing me both to this facet of Mariology and to Rahner's wonderful little book.

body was "born of woman," so also must His mystical body be "born of woman" if, as Saint Paul says in Romans 8, we are to be heirs of all that is His.

That is why Saint Augustine can say that no one can have God for his Father who does not have the Church for his mother. He was expressing no more than the immediate intuition, common to all believers, that the Church is the mother of those who are born anew in Christ. The Church did not just learn to be a mother from Mary, but mystically continues the mothering of Mary by giving birth to Christ's brothers and sisters (cf. Rom. 8:29).

Heart of the Matter

The Marian character of the Church has always found artistic expression in the placing of Mary at the center of the gathered disciples on Pentecost. Some Christians who do not accept the place of Mary in the economy of salvation say that Mary is only mentioned in passing as being among the followers of Jesus in the biblical account of Pentecost. But while Luke only glancingly mentions the presence of Mary in the midst of the apostles, holy women, and brethren in Acts 1:14, the representation of Mary at center stage of the drama of Pentecost is more than just a Catholic interpolation that makes more of her role than the scriptural evidence warrants.

Rather, by virtue of that same familial instinct expressed by Augustine and so many other theologians, the Church knows where a mother ought to be and where a sinless mother would certainly be—in the midst of her children. And, in fact, Luke's narratives of the Annunciation and Visitation almost demand that we put Mary at the center on Pentecost.

Saint Luke draws clear parallels between the ministry of Christ in his Gospel and the ministry of the Church in his Acts of the Apostles. His intent seems to be to show the continuity between Christ and the Body of Christ, the Church, a theme he likely would have heard Saint Paul voice on more than one occasion. Indeed, Luke is the one who records Christ speaking of Himself and the Church as one in Paul's vision on the road to

Damascus in Acts 9:5: "I am Jesus, whom you are persecuting."
There is another hint of this continuity in the prologue of Acts,
in which Luke tells us that his first work, the Gospel he had
already written, "dealt with all that Jesus *began* to do and
teach" (Acts 1:1). The implication is that what Christ began in
His earthly body He will continue in His mystical body, the
Church. Acts does in fact show us the Church continuing what
Jesus began.

Luke is the only evangelist who records the scene of the
Annunciation, that moment, called the Incarnation, when the
earthly body of Christ took form under the heart of Mary. We
ought, then, to expect to see in Acts the Incarnation of the
Mystical Body of Christ. And that is what we find in the
Pentecost story. The significant difference between these two
incarnations is a matter of physical location. The human body of
Christ took shape *within* Mary by the work of the Holy Spirit at
the Incarnation. On Pentecost, the Mystical Body of Christ took
shape *around* Mary.[10]

We find a similar event in the account of the Visitation, a kind
of post-Incarnation and pre-Pentecost which simultaneously
looks back to the Incarnation of the human body of Christ and
forward to the incarnation of the Mystical Body of Christ at
Pentecost. Saint Luke tells us that

---

[10] We can find here wonderful food for meditation in a typological conjunction of the
association of Mary as daughter Zion, the place of the Temple in Jerusalem, and the
image from Hebrews 9 and 10 of Jesus as the one high priest who is alone able to enter
into the Holy of Holies. The author of Hebrews specifically quotes Psalm 40:6,
"Sacrifices and offerings thou hast not desired, but a body hast thou prepared for me"
(Heb. 10:5). Just as according to the Old Law only the high priest could enter into the
Holy of Holies in the temple, so also only the one true high priest was able to enter into
the Holy of Holies that was Mary. By doing so He received, through the mediation of
Mary, the body by which He would serve as *the* Mediator between God and man. (Even
Mary's subordinate mediation on the physical level is dependent on His divine power.)
Note that in the Pentecost narrative the rest of the priests (apostles) and people (disci-
ples) of the new Israel must remain in the outer courts of the Marian temple that the
upper room and its environs have become.

when Elizabeth heard the greeting of Mary, the babe leaped in her
womb; and Elizabeth was filled with the Holy Spirit and she
exclaimed with a loud cry, "Blessed are you among women, and
blessed is the fruit of your womb!" (Lk. 1:41-42).

Elizabeth and John receive the Holy Spirit in the first reception of that Spirit after the overshadowing of Mary at the
Incarnation. As Peter will later be seen to do at Pentecost,
Elizabeth is immediately moved to cry out, to proclaim the
good news, the Gospel. She does so in a way that has become
characteristic of the Marian Church: "Blessed are you among
women, and blessed is the fruit of your womb." Here we see, in
a kind of mini-Pentecost, the Church, the Body of Christ, first
formed in miniature *around* Mary just after the body of Christ
has been formed *in* Mary at the Annunciation.

But despite the difference in physical location, the mystical
location of the Mystical Body of Christ is the same as that of the
human body of Jesus—under the heart of the Mary. She is the
New Eve, the mother of all the living. It is by her singular
maternal mediation, by "the greeting of Mary," that all those
born into the body of Christ receive the life that comes
through the Holy Spirit. This mediation is possible because she
conceived the origin of all saving grace by the overshadowing
of the Holy Spirit.

We see here, in seminal form, a scriptural expression of the
Catholic belief that Mary is the mediatrix of all graces, which is,
after all, a corollary to the doctrine of the Marian Church. She
conceives Christ by the Holy Spirit at the Incarnation and brings
Christ in the Spirit to Elizabeth and John. Her role as mediatrix
is first expressed when her body has been shown to be a temple
of the Holy Spirit at the Annunciation. Christ, the one high
priest, enters into the Holy of Holies, the one who is "full of
grace." She then bears Him to Elizabeth and John, who leaps
with joy at the sound of her voice. It certainly could have been
otherwise. God could have made a visitation Himself by some
sort of direct spiritual manifestation. But the whole import of the

Incarnation is that God has chosen to take on flesh for His purposes, to enlist our aid, though He does not need it. The
Church of Christ, born of the Holy Spirit at Pentecost, but born
first in miniature at the Visitation, is that Church where Mary is
at the center. In fact, it is that Church where Mary is the Church,
or rather the Church is fully Marian.

Breadth of the Mystery

Is this all a lot of confusion, a Catholic complexification, a
muddling of the proper roles in what should be a well-ordered
scheme of simple, clear relationships? No, it is but one expression
of a divine mystery that is stubbornly multiform. The nub of this
mystery is that God has invited mere humans, and in this case
particularly a humble virgin from Nazareth, to participate in the
plan of the mystery and thus become "partakers of the divine
nature" (2 Pet. 1:4). As He is Himself a whole sea of mystery, we
ought not to be surprised if our own lives also get caught up in
this great Marian mystery (cf. Eph. 5:32).

The mystery of Mary and the Marian Church is vast. We have
only approached this mystery, immense enough to "encompass"
the whole economy of salvation, just from the aspect of Mary's
and the Church's mutual maternity.[11] She is also daughter, virgin,
bride, and spouse before—and even after—she gives birth as
mother. And a mother doesn't just give birth to her child; she also
cares for him, feeds him, and teaches him. These are all aspects
of the mothering of Mary and the Church that we have not even
touched upon. What a vast horizon of meditation is opened up to
us when we enter into the Marian womb of the Church! But a

---

[11] See Jeremiah 31:21-22. This mysterious passage, preceding the promise of a New
Covenant and addressed to "virgin Israel," announces that "the LORD has created a new
thing on the earth: a woman protects a man." The New American Bible translates verse
22: "The LORD has created a new thing upon the earth: the woman must *encompass* the
man with devotion" (emphasis added).

fully Catholic, which is to say *Marian,* statement of the breadth
of this mystery was perhaps best made by Gerard Manley
Hopkins in that poem evocatively titled, "The Blessed Virgin
compared to the Air we Breathe":

> I say that we are wound
> With mercy round and round
> As if with air: the same
> Is Mary, more by name.
> She, wild web, wondrous robe,
> Mantles the guilty globe,
> Since God has let dispense
> Her prayers his providence:
> Nay, more than almoner,
> The sweet alms' self is her
> And men are meant to share
> Her life as life does air.[12]

*Sean Innerst is provost of St. John Vianney Theological
Seminary in Denver. A convert to the Catholic faith from the
Society of Friends or Quakers, he edits and writes for a variety
of Catholic publications, is a contributor to the* Encyclopedia of
Catholic Doctrine *(Our Sunday Visitor, 1997), and is preparing
a catechetical commentary on the Sunday Lectionary based on
the Catechism.*

---

[12] As reproduced in F.J. Sheed, ed., *The Mary Book* (New York: Sheed & Ward, 1950),
244-47.

CHAPTER XI

The Rosary

It Beats the Rhythm of Human Life

JEFFERY CAVINS

Some of my non-Catholic Christian friends worry that the Rosary is an "extra-biblical prayer." "If it is extra-biblical," they say, "it is man-made." Yet, the idea of God's revelation coming to us from the Bible alone is itself a teaching you cannot find in the Bible! The truth is that the Word of God has historically come to us in both written and unwritten form. Did this start with the Catholic Church? Actually it started a little bit earlier: about 1400 B.C. on Mount Sinai. The Jews believed that God's Word, the Torah, came to Moses in written form—the five books of Moses—and it came in unwritten form, later to be written down as the Talmud.[1] So the Jews understood the Word of God to be both written and unwritten.

Many people will say at this point, "But the Jews were just wrong to think this way. After all, Jesus condemned all tradition

[1] Rabbi Hayim Donin, *To Be a Jew: A Guide to Jewish Observance in Contemporary Life* (New York: Basic Books, 1972), 24-25.

in Mark 7:8 when He rebuked the Pharisees by saying, "You leave the commandment of God, and hold fast the tradition of men." But this is to misread Jesus. For Jesus did not condemn *all* tradition; He condemned confusing the traditions of men with the Tradition of God. How do we know? Because Jesus teaches from both the written Torah *and* the unwritten Torah, like all good rabbis. That is why Jesus can refer to the teaching office in Israel by the title "Moses' Seat" (Mt. 23:2), even though that title exists nowhere in the Old Testament and is only found in Jewish tradition. It is also why Jesus makes free use of preexisting stories and parables in Jewish tradition and adapts them to His own purposes, such as the parable of the Good Samaritan in Luke 10, which is adapted from a rabbinic tale preserved in the Tosefta (Yom HaKipurim 1:12).

In short, Jesus honors the concept of the unwritten Torah. He distinguishes, not between Tradition and Scripture, but between human tradition and God's Tradition. So does the Church He founds. That is why Saint Paul tells the Thessalonians to "stand firm and hold to the traditions which you were taught by us, either by word of mouth or by letter" (2 Thess. 2:15). So when the Church is established, the Church understands that the early disciples are to share the *full* deposit of faith that Jesus gave them, which is also both written and unwritten.

Where, then, did Jesus place His authority first and foremost? In a book? How could He have? After all, Scripture was not all written for at least sixty years after the Church was in operation, and it was not assembled into something resembling its final form for nearly three centuries after that. Rather, Jesus placed His authority in the Church to share all that He has revealed. Jesus says to His disciples in Matthew 16, "Who do men say that the Son of man is?" (v. 13). They reply, "Some say John the Baptist, others say Elijah, and others Jeremiah or one of the prophets" (v. 14). Jesus then says, "But who do *you* say that I am?" (v. 15), and Peter looks at Christ and says, "You are the Christ, the Son of the living God" (v. 16). And Jesus says:

Blessed are you, Simon Bār-Jona! For flesh and blood has not revealed this to you, but my Father who is in heaven. And I tell you, you are Peter, and on this rock I will build my church. . . . I will give you the keys of the kingdom of heaven, and whatever you bind on earth shall be bound in heaven, and whatever you loose on earth shall be loosed in heaven (Mt. 16:17-19).

"Binding and loosing" is a rabbinic term of the first century. It means that Jesus is so intimate with Peter and the Church that He says, "Whatever you allow, Peter, I'm allowing. Whatever you don't allow, I am not allowing." In other words, He meant business when He told Peter and His Church, "He who hears you hears me, and he who rejects you rejects me, and he who rejects me rejects him who sent me" (Lk. 10:16).

So the whole issue of where teachings and doctrines come from goes back to authority. If the authority to decide what is and is not the authentic teaching of Christ lies with the individual, then we can all make up doctrines and give interpretations. But if the authority is in the Church and that authority comes from Christ Himself (as He promised in Luke 10:16), then in every official teaching of the Church you can count on hearing Jesus. When the Church says, "This is truth," you can say, "Yes, Lord! I hear you, because God has placed His authority there and Jesus said, 'When you hear the Church, you hear me.'"

It is within the Catholic Church and by her authority from Christ that the Rosary is given to us. But, of course, it is one thing to give and quite another to receive. I am a revert, someone who has come back to the Catholic Church after several years away. I had a rosary as a child but, though I was *given* a rosary, I never really *received* it. I did not know how to pray it or what it was for. I remember sitting on the edge of my bed when I was about four years old, pretending it was the reins of a horse's bridle. That was about the extent of my use for it.

I have since fallen in love with the Rosary. The Rosary has become the circle of my life. Through this special prayer, I am able to come to know and love Christ in a more intimate way.

What Is the Rosary?

According to the popes, the Rosary is *the most highly rec-ommended prayer in the Catholic Church, second only to the liturgy*.[2] I think one of the reasons for this high recommendation is that it is a quick way for us to enter the world of Jesus and meditate on the most precious Gospels. It focuses on the greatest Gospel mysteries, from the Annunciation on through to the Death and Resurrection of Our Lord and concluding with the Crowning of Our Lady. Pope Paul VI says it is a "compendium of the entire Gospel."[3] It is an orderly and gradual unfolding of the way God entered human affairs.

Saint Paul gives us a kind of synopsis of the Rosary when he writes:

> Have this mind among yourselves, which was in Christ Jesus, who, though he was in the form of God, did not count equality with God a thing to be grasped, but emptied himself, taking the form of a servant, being born in the likeness of men. And being found in human form he humbled himself and became obedient unto death, even death on a cross. Therefore God has highly exalted him and bestowed on him the name which is above every name, that at the name of Jesus every knee should bow, in heaven and on earth and under the earth, and every tongue confess that Jesus Christ is Lord, to the glory of God the Father (Phil. 2:5-11).

Jesus came as a man, He suffered death, and in the end, He was highly exalted. That is the Rosary in a nutshell.

The Rosary consists of fifteen sets of ten Hail Marys, referred to as decades, with an Our Father prayed at the beginning of each decade. During the praying of each decade, one of the central mysteries of the Gospel is meditated upon (we will return to this

---

[2] Cf. Pope Paul VI, Apostolic Exhortation Devotion to the Blessed Virgin Mary *Marialis Cultus* (1974), no. 54.
[3] *Ibid.*, no. 42.

in a moment). In all, there are fifteen Our Fathers, 150 Hail Marys, coupled with—mark this—vocal prayer (at least a movement of the lips). Why the insistence on *that*? Because the whole prayer is about the drama of the Word made *flesh*, not the Word made thought. So we enter into the spirit of the prayer, with our *bodies* just as Jesus entered into our salvation with His body.

This incarnational aspect cannot be stressed too much. You and I are created in what may be called a "dynamic unity." We are spirit *and* body. The Rosary reflects this dynamic unity by involving the body in the fingering of the beads and the spirit in meditating and praying about the mysteries of Jesus Christ. Head *and* heart, soul *and* body therefore participate in the Rosary.

The Rosary is also a practical prayer. As we count the beads with our hands, the soul is freed from the practical distraction of counting. The physical involvement of the body, coupled with the physical formation of the words, keeps the body at the disposition of the soul. Have you ever found your mind wandering off into the ozone during prayer? Prayer can be tiring. But there is something about the touching of the beads that keeps our bodies focused. I like what one author said: "[T]he beads are there for the sake of the prayers, and the prayers are there for the sake of the Mysteries"[4] that we are meditating upon.

After World War I, doctors noticed that much of the tension that had built up in the returning soldiers was alleviated through using their hands. That is why one of the therapies they recommended for World War I veterans was knitting. Tension and anxiety will often leave our bodies through our hands. So it is interesting that our mother Mary has asked us to involve our hands in meditation.

[4] Maisie Ward, *The Splendor of the Rosary* (New York: Sheed and Ward, 1945), 11-12, as quoted by Mark Miravalle, *Introduction to Mary* (Santa Barbara, CA: Queenship Publishing Company, 1993), 97.

The Origins of the Rosary

One tradition tells us that the Rosary came from Saint Dominic Guzman around the year 1221. Saint Dominic had been to southern France to preach against the Albigensian heresy, which denied the goodness of creation and held that the spirit is good but that matter (including the body) is evil. A common saying in Albigensianism was "the body is a tomb," suggesting that true freedom is realized only when one is freed from the flesh. This heresy held that there are two supreme beings: a good god who created the spirit world, and an evil god who created the material world. Since matter was evil to the Albigensians, marriage and procreation were evil. Jesus was not thought to be human, nor was Mary considered the mother of God. Albigensianism denied the humanity of Christ. The Crucifixion and Resurrection of Jesus were only illusions, and the whole concept of the cross in the Christian life was rejected.

The story goes that Mary came to Saint Dominic and gave him the Rosary to combat this heresy. Whatever the historical merits of the story, the fact is if you look at the structure of the Rosary—the Joyful Mysteries (the birth and childhood of Jesus), the Sorrowful Mysteries (the suffering of Jesus), and the Glorious Mysteries (the bodily Resurrection and Ascension of Jesus and His exaltation of Mary)—you see the wisdom of Mary in combating the ideas of this heresy, ideas which are as common today as in the twelfth century.

Albigensianism, like many newer religious fads, discounted the fact that divinity intersected with humanity in Christ. In contrast to this dualism, the prayers of the Rosary continually focus on the reality of the Incarnation. So, for example, the Hail Mary says in part, "Blessed art thou among women, and blessed is the *fruit of thy womb*, Jesus." These words express our belief that God the Son truly became one like us. So Saint Dominic would go into the villages and would preach to them the mysteries of salvation and then pray the Hail Marys. The Hail Marys constitute "the warp on which is woven the contemplation of the mysteries."[5] It is on those Hail Marys that we weave in the life of Christ and meditate on Jesus, the God-man. The Rosary then developed over the years until, in 1569, Pope St. Pius V officially approved the current form.

People say, "1569!? Isn't that a little bit late?" But we have to remember a point John Henry Cardinal Newman made in his *Essay On The Development of Christian Doctrine*. He said God has given us the truth, but over the years the Church's understanding develops and grows. Though there is no new revelation, we *grow* in our understanding of what God has given us, and the Rosary is one great expression of the growth of the Tradition. The idea of development or growth is not a novelty of Cardinal Newman's. He got it from Our Lord, who said:

> The kingdom of heaven is like a grain of mustard seed which a man took and sowed in his field; it is the smallest of all seeds, but when it has grown it is the greatest of shrubs and becomes a tree, so that the birds of the air come and make nests in its branches (Mt. 13:31-32).

Doctrine, like the mustard seed, grows. But it never mutates because God is the One who causes the growth.

Entering Mary's Worldview

One of the things I appreciate most about the Rosary is its flexibility. No matter how simple or complex our lives are, we can pray with the Rosary and never exhaust its riches. The same holds true with the Scriptures and the Tradition of the Church. We will never exhaust them. We are so blessed as Catholics because we have been placed in an atmosphere which can con-

---

[5] Pope John Paul II, Angelus Message, October 26, 1997, as reproduced in *L'Osservatore Romano* (English ed., October 29, 1997), 1.

tinually nourish us! As Peter wrote, "His divine power has granted to us all things that pertain to life and godliness, through the knowledge of him who called us to his own glory and excellence" (2 Pet. 1:3).

It has been said that the Rosary is shallow enough that an ant can wade in it and deep enough that an elephant can drown in it. If you are just beginning your walk in Christ, the Rosary will offer you the simplest walk through His life. But even if you have been walking with Christ for years, you still will not exhaust the mysteries of Christ: You still will not exhaust all the revelation that God wants to give you about His life and your condition through the eyes of Mary.

Pope John Paul II says, "The Rosary is my favorite prayer, a marvelous prayer; marvelous in its simplicity and marvelous in its depth."[6] He adds that the Rosary "beats the rhythm of human life."[7] What does he mean by that?

If you think about the way the Rosary is put together, no matter what condition or circumstance you are in, you can find yourself in it.

It starts with the mystery of the Annunciation: the announcement that God is going to come into people's lives in a new way. That happens in my life, sometimes on a weekly basis. When I meditate on the mystery of the angel coming to Mary, I often tie it into my own life and see that God wants to do a new thing in my marriage or with my children. We recently adopted a little girl. She is so beautiful! And I think about a brand new beginning for the Cavins household as I meditate on the mystery of the Annunciation. I say, "Lord, you come to give us the good news, and there is the opportunity to start over here."

---

[6] Pope John Paul II, Angelus Message, October 29, 1978, as reproduced in *L'Osservatore Romano* (English ed., November 9, 1978), 2.
[7] *Ibid.*

The Rosary proceeds through the Visitation, where we discover Jesus in our neighbor as Elizabeth discovered Him in Mary, and on to the Nativity, the birth of Christ in *our* lives. There is the Presentation in the Temple, where we present ourselves to God, and the Finding of Christ, where we find Christ teaching and studying in the Temple even as a boy.

Then, moving from that new beginning period of the Joyful Mysteries, we move into the Sorrowful Mysteries. Here, we begin to confront some of the hard realities of life. You do not say, "Isn't it wonderful?" when you are on the cross. The Rosary calls us to see the joy in life and enjoy it, but it also forces us to confront the suffering in life and bear the cross. Maybe you had a little boy, and he was full of snakes and snails and puppy dog tails. It was all Joyful Mysteries in those years. But now he is entering high school and you are coming up against a sorrowful world full of drugs, sex, guns, and gangs. Maybe there are some difficult times with a marriage that once was joyful, and you are really struggling. Or maybe it is your job, or something somebody said to you, or health problems. Whatever the case, there is nothing you must face alone, for Jesus Christ faced His own sorrows—and ours—when He endured the Agony in the Garden, the Scourging at the Pillar, the Crowning with Thorns, the Carrying of the Cross, and His Death on the Cross.

Nor must you think life ends there. For the Rosary shouts, "There is hope!" and continues on to the Glorious Mysteries of the Resurrection, the Ascension, Pentecost, the Assumption, and the Coronation of Mary. In these Glorious Mysteries, the Rosary shows us what will become of us in the future. It declares the message of the Son of God Himself that there is hope, glory, and joy for the future and that we *do* have something to look forward to!

And so, no matter where we are in life, we can find ourselves somewhere in the Rosary. As Pope John Paul II says:

At the same time our heart can enclose in these decades of the
Rosary all the facts that make up the life of the individual, the
family, the nation, the Church, and mankind. Personal matters
and those of one's neighbor, and particularly of those who are
closest to us, who are dearest to us.[8]

Maybe in our marriage we are struggling through the
Sorrowful Mysteries; maybe with our children, we are in the
midst of the Joyful Mysteries; maybe in our vocation, we are
somewhere in the Glorious Mysteries. Wherever we are in our
lives, we can meditate on these mysteries and allow Mary to show
us the life of Christ in a new dimension. Not only did Mary
watch Jesus go through each phase of His life, she was *with* Him
every step of the way, experiencing it all with her own body. In
her own heart she experienced the joy, the sorrow, and the glory.
She has been crowned Queen of Heaven by her Son.

Likewise, you and I, Scripture says, will one day receive
crowns that we will in turn throw down at the feet of Jesus (cf.
1 Pet. 5:4; Rev. 4:9-11). Like Mary, we will experience the
Joyful, Sorrowful, and Glorious Mysteries on a personal scale.

Repetition and the Rhythm of Life

Some Christians will object that, according to Scripture,
Jesus was against repetitious prayer. However, Jesus warned
against *meaningless* repetition, not *meaningful* repetition.
Meaningless repetition is indeed not God's will. Merely rattling
off prayers like a parrot will not move the hand of God. But
not all repetition is meaningless. When people tell me it is, I
sometimes suggest they pinch their nose shut and clamp their
lips tightly together. Within seconds, they begin to notice the
life-giving value of repetition.

Romano Guardini discussed the issue with that logic and
wrote:

---

[8] *Ibid.*

[R]epetition can have a real meaning. Is it not an element of all life? What else is the beating of the heart but a repetition? Always the same contraction and expansion—and yet it makes the blood circulate through the body. What else is breathing but a repetition? Always the same in and out—but by breathing we live. And is not our whole being ordered and sustained by change and repetition? Ever anew the sun rises and sets, night follows day; the round of life begins in the spring, rises, reaches its summit, and sinks. What objection can one raise against these repetitions and so many others? They are the order in which growth progresses, the inner kernel develops, and the form is revealed. All life realizes itself in the rhythm of external conditions and internal accomplishment. If this is so everywhere, why should it not also be so in religious devotion?[9]

Isn't every day a matter of getting up, going to work, eating lunch, coming home, eating dinner, kids doing this, kids doing that? Are not our lives repetitious? Understandably then, the God of life, all throughout the Old Testament, said, "Establish this feast in *this* month and every year when you come to this month, do this. And every year at *that* month, do that" (cf. Lev. 23). Every day, the Jews would pray three times the Sh'ma: "Hear, O Israel: The LORD our God is one LORD" (Deut. 6:4).

God thus enters our daily routine with His power. The divine intersects the mundane! That is why I love the Catholic Church's liturgical year and its cycle of readings. Every three years we get selections from the whole Bible! Every year, we go through the entire life of Christ in our readings at weekday Masses. We need this. It is breathing in and breathing out.

So if I find the Rosary boring, it is probably because I'm not entering into the Rosary. I am just repeating words instead of entering into it and meditating on the life of Christ through the eyes of Mary. That is why I like to think of each bead as the heartbeat of Jesus, and my goal is that my heart would beat in unison with His.

---

[9] Romano Guardini, *The Rosary of Our Lady* (Manchester, NH: Sophia Institute, 1983), 17-18.

As soon as a person begins praying the words of the creed, Guardini wrote, "[H]e has built for himself a home by his speech."[10] Think of the endless possibilities to experience intimacy with the Lord. We can pray on the way to work, transforming traffic jams into meaningful times of prayer. We sit down in the doctor's waiting room, take out our rosary, and we build ourselves a home, a sanctuary in time. There is no place or situation in which we cannot erect a place of pondering. We need such a place of holy tranquility. We need a place where we can go to get away from it all, where the breath of God pervades, and where we can meet the great figures of the faith: Jesus, Mary, and the apostles. As Guardini wrote, "The Rosary is not a road, but a place, and it has no goal but a depth. To linger in it has great compensations."[11] It is not some task that we busy Americans have to accomplish, but a lingering in the world of Mary, whose mission was to bear Christ to the world. Mary is the bridge between the Old and New Testaments. What better person to go to and say, "You know the old and you know the new. Explain the Christ to me and draw me to His Sacred Heart."

Meditating on the Rosary

As we noted earlier, no one knows Jesus like Mary. After the angel came to Mary in the Annunciation, Luke 2:19 tells us that Mary "kept all these things, pondering them in her heart." In the Rosary, you and I are doing what our mother Mary did.

Why do we say she is *our* mother? It is commonly understood that anything that happens at the foot of the Cross is a universal event. In other words, if it happened at the Cross, it applies to all Christians. And so, for instance, all of us are washed in the blood shed on the Cross. Similarly, it was at the Cross that Jesus said to Mary, "Woman, behold, your son!" (Jn. 19:26) and to the beloved

---

[10] *Ibid.*, 28.
[11] *Ibid.*, 45.

disciple (and what Christian is not His beloved disciple?),
"Behold, your mother!" (Jn. 19:27). From Calvary, "her
motherhood has extended to the brothers and sisters of her
Son 'who still journey on earth surrounded by dangers and
difficulties'" (Catechism, no. 2674, quoting LG 62).

So Jesus gives His mother to the Church as *our* mother, to
watch over us, to pray for us, to intercede for us as the Mediatrix
of All Graces. She is in no way divine, but she has a very special
place given to us by Christ. She did not take this place herself; it
was appointed for her and for us by Christ.

In John 2, at the wedding at Cana, we see Mary in the role
of mediatrix. Someone may object that Scripture says, "[T]here
is one mediator between God and men, the man Christ Jesus"
(1 Tim. 2:5). True. But Scripture also says Christ is our one
teacher (Mt. 23:8). It does not therefore follow that there can
be no other teachers, for Saint Paul tells us that Christ has
given us other teachers (Eph. 4:11). So the word "one" has the
sense of "primary" rather than "sole" here. Mary therefore
shares in Christ's work of mediation just as teachers share in
His work of teaching.

All Christians participate in Christ's one mediation. That's
why when people come up to me and say, "Listen, I know you
and Emily have a strong marriage, so I would like to ask you to
pray for me," I don't whirl around and say, "Hey, there is only one
mediator so don't come to me!" We all understand the reality that
we can and should pray for one another with the power that
Jesus shares with us by the Holy Spirit. It is the same with Mary.
What we are doing is saying, "Mother, will you please pray for
me? Nobody knows your Son like you do."

Someone asks, "But should you be praying to people who are
no longer on earth?" Yes. The Body of Christ cannot be divided.
The fact that our loved ones have gone before us, that we have
the saints as our older brothers and sisters, does not mean that we
are separated. We are one body in Jesus Christ. As Saint Paul says,
we are members, not only of Christ Jesus but "one of another"
(Rom. 12:5). Those who have gone before us have not suddenly

become supernaturally stupid. They know what is happening here, and we can have a relationship with them and ask them to pray for us. As Orthodox Christians like to say, "The saints see us reflected in God's eyes."

And so John takes us to the wedding at Cana and writes:

> On the third day there was a marriage at Cana in Galilee, and the mother of Jesus was there; Jesus also was invited to the marriage, with his disciples. When the wine failed, the mother of Jesus said to him, "They have no wine" (Jn. 2:1-3).

In this little story we learn so much about Mary. Mary's unique mediation has a maternal dimension. She comes to us in the wide variety of our wants and needs, and she brings these wants and needs to Jesus Christ.

Pope John Paul II says in his encyclical *Redemptoris Mater*:

> In John's text on the other hand, the description of the Cana event outlines what is actually manifested as a new kind of motherhood according to the spirit and not just according to the flesh, that is to say *Mary's solicitude for human beings*, her coming to them in the wide variety of their wants and needs. At Cana in Galilee there is shown only one concrete aspect of human need, apparently a small one of little importance ("They have no wine"). But it has a symbolic value: this coming to the aid of human needs means, at the same time, bringing those needs within the radius of Christ's messianic mission and salvific power. Thus there is a mediation: Mary places herself between her Son and mankind in the reality of their wants, needs and sufferings. *She puts herself "in the middle,"* that is to say *she acts as a mediatrix not as an outsider, but in her position as mother.*[12]

---

[12] Pope John Paul II, Encyclical Letter Mother of the Redeemer *Redemptoris Mater* (1986), no. 21, original emphasis.

Mary brings the mundane things of our lives into the radius of Christ's mission and power! She brings the things that you and I would have thought uninteresting to Jesus. She voluntarily steps into the middle between Christ and us and says, "These are the needs they have." But though she volunteers, she does so because Our Father—who "knows what you need before you ask him" (Mt. 6:8)—wills it. He desires to spread His joy in caring for His creatures and honors Mary with that joy. And so Mary lives out not a role or duty but a *love*: She delightedly acts like the mother she is because God in His power and omniscience delights to have it so. He is a not a doddering old man who needs Mary to remind Him for us. But we are little children who need her maternal care—something we can learn here on earth from our own mothers if we pay attention.

When I was a child, we would drive to see my grandparents, and I could count on my mother turning around at some point, taking a handkerchief, and cleaning me up in order to see Grandma and Grandpa. In the same way, when we are about to encounter some difficulty in our lives, Mary our mother says, "Come here. You have some things in your life that need to be cleaned up. I see what they are and you do not. You might squirm, but I love you, and my Son, the King of Kings, has given me responsibility for you." The thing I appreciate about Mary is that she is our mother and—let's face it—there is a difference between a mother's prayers and anyone else's when it comes to her children's needs. Mothers do not miss anything. They see the details of their children's lives.

Likewise, as the Holy Father says, we see Mary take the most mundane things and bring them into Christ's radius. When I pray the Rosary, I am so aware as I am praying that this is my *mother* interceding for me, and there are things in my life, not that *God* does not see, but that *I* do not see.

It is such a privilege to know that not only am I serving the King of Kings, but also that He has given me a mother. So, let's not be afraid to pray about the mundane things of our lives as we pray the Rosary. That is what Mary is concerned with.

Practical Suggestions

The biblical idea of meditation is the same idea as a cow chewing her cud. A cow takes in the hay, chews it, swallows it down to one stomach, brings it up again, and chews it more. The cow gets all she can out of it. In the same way, in meditating on the mysteries of the Rosary, there are three simple but important things to remember:

1. Consider the mystery. Carefully rehearse the event in your thinking.
2. Apply the mystery. Apply the truths to your life. Ask questions of that mystery.
3. Resolve. Make some practical decision to *do* something about the mystery as it applies in your life.

With that in mind, ask yourself, "What are some of the areas in my life for which I need Mary's mediation and her prayers?" No matter how small they are, she sees them and wants to bring them to the Lord. So, as you finish reading this chapter, take a moment and think about those areas of your life that you might like to submit to her for prayer. In the same way, take a little while and think about where you are on the timeline of the Rosary. As you meditate, pray. Perhaps pause a little between beads and say, "Lord, I really need your help here." Talk to Him a little bit. Expect God to make Himself known to you somehow. It may not be spectacular, but that's okay. Most of life does not make your heart race, but rather passes with a steady, regular beat: the rhythm of the human—and the Sacred—heart.

Jeffery Cavins is a popular conference speaker on Scripture and apologetics, and is the host of "Life on the Rock," a weekly television program produced by the Eternal Word Television Network. He resides in Maple Grove, Minnesota, with his wife Emily and their three children.

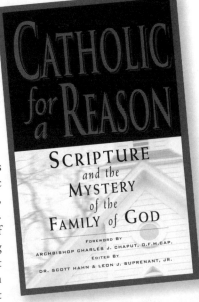